Strang

True Stories
of Garrett County

Garrett County
Historical Society

McClain Printing Company
212 Main Street
Parsons, WV 26287
http://McClainPrinting.com

International Standard Book Number 0-87012-640-7
Printed in the United States of America
Published by the Garrett County Historical Society
Oakland, Maryland
All Rights Reserved
2000

Front Cover: Pictured is a section of Oakland High School that was located at the corner of Green and Fifth streets (now a parking lot for the Garrett County Board of Education). The structure originally served as the first Garrett County Jail, and it was in this jail yard that John Smith was hanged on November 16, 1883, for the murder of Josiah Harden. It was the only execution ever to take place in Garrett County.

Acknowledgments

The Garrett County Historical Society, Inc. wishes to thank all those who loaned pictures, gave information and offered encouragement in this project.

Research, information and material gathered from:
Garrett County Board of Education
Ruth Enlow Library
The *Republican* newspaper–Permission granted by Don Sincell, editor
Files from the library of The Garrett County Historical Society, Inc.
The *Glades Star*, a quarterly publication of The Garrett County Historical Society, John Grant, editor

Some of these stories have been extracted from articles written by:
R. Getty Browning
Ross C. Durst
Francis Turner
H. Wayne Wilt

and published in various volumes of The *Glades Star*.

Compiled by The Garrett County Historical Society Publication Committee John Grant, Chairman, Martha Kahl and Dorothy Cathell.

Table of Contents

The Murder of Josiah Harden

Garrett County's
Only Criminal Execution
by H. Wayne Wilt

Location of execution was at far corner of present Board of Education parking lot.

"Editor's Note: Mr. Wilt wrote the following article after researching the records, and has given it as a talk to various community groups.

This is the case of:

The State of Maryland

vs.

John Herbert Smith

"Mr. Smith is part of Garrett County history because he was the first person to commit murder in this county, since it was formed in 1872. He was also the first person to be executed by hanging in the county.

"The murder occurred on May 15, 1883, when Garrett County was only eleven years old, and the offense was committed near Elkins, better known as Gorman.

"Mr. Smith was a black man about 40-years-old, who was born in Harrisonburg, and was sold as a slave on two different occasions in the state of Virginia. At a certain age he was allowed to leave his slave owner to live an independent life. He left home against the advice of his mother, and later he regretted ignoring her advice.

"Mr. Smith appeared to be a hard worker. He was employed on the railroad in Harrisonburg and had worked in Washington, DC and Baltimore for the water department. On one occasion while travelling from Washington to Alexandria, VA, he was robbed of his money and he immediately returned to Washington, where he obtained employment lighting lamps. In 1875, he obtained employment with the Chesapeake and Ohio Railroad, and in 1881, he went to Piedmont, and in 1882, he moved to Elkins (Gorman) and obtained employment as a foreman on railroad construction.

"The victim was Josiah Harden. For quite sometime The *Republican* newspaper referred to him as Josiah Harding. He was about 55-years-old, white, married with five children, a native of Garrett County and resided in the Gorman area. He served in the Confederate Army and was self-employed as a shoemaker, and was a former resident of Accident. Mr. Harden was known to have some legal problems. He had been in jail on a charge of attempting to negotiate a forged check and escaped from jail, but he was not considered a vicious person.

"Mr. Smith and Mr. Harden appeared to be friends. Smith was a frequent visitor at the Harden residence, and Harden was beginning to question why Smith was visiting his home. Later, many people believed that Mrs. Harden and her mother had encouraged Smith's visits.

"On the day of the murder, which was May 15, 1883, Mr. Smith had been drinking and making threats against various people. He had told someone that he was going to leave Elkins (Gorman) the next day, but before leaving he would do something that would make the people of Elkins remember that day forever. Smith went looking for Harden. At a saloon, he approached and looked very closely at Benjamin Miller, then said, 'You are not the S.O.B. that I'm looking for.' He made it quite clear that he was looking for Harden.

"Upon leaving Elkins, Smith went to the Harden residence, arriving between 6 and 7 pm, and remained there until 8 pm, holding conversation with various family members. He paid Harden 5 cents for repairing his boots, and while there, he made a statement to Harden's son, Robert, 'Your father don't like me very much.' He also stated that he had a present for every member of the family, and he was going away, but would return in 30 minutes to hand out the gifts.

"It appeared that Smith wanted to give a present to every member of the Harden family. He inquired as to whether Harden's oldest son and son-in-law would be home later in the evening. He was assured that these gentlemen would not be home. He continued to promise gifts, stating that he had a nice instrument in his pocket, which makes nice music, but he would not have as much fun as he expected since the Harden relatives were away.

"Smith continued to be friendly and he asked Harden to have a drink of whiskey, but Harden refused by saying, 'It was bed time' and he 'wanted to go to bed.' Smith encouraged him to go to bed, but Harden, using his manners, felt it wouldn't be polite to go to bed with Smith visiting his home. So, Smith left and went on his way.

"About 30 minutes later, Mr. Harden was sitting with his back toward a window and his 9-year-old daughter was sleeping in the same room. Mrs. Harden and two other children were sitting beside Mr. Harden. Without warning, someone shot two times through the window, striking Mr. Harden. He jumped up, shook his hand, felt his shoulder and said, 'Don't do that Smith. Don't do that anymore. That's enough of that.' Harden feeling that his family may be endangered told them to run upstairs, and he started toward the door to confront Smith. Smith, breaking open the door met Harden and a scuffle took place. Smith fired three more shots striking Harden in the back and neck. He was shot five times.

"The family members remained upstairs, and feared for their personal safety. Mr. Harden, dying from the wounds was unable to protect his home and family. Smith realizing that he had things under control, ran upstairs, grabbed Mrs. Harden and forced her into the woods where he raped her. Robert Harden, age 15, attempted to protect his mother, struck Smith on the head with a gun, but Smith pointed a gun at Robert and he ran back into the house.

"Upon Mrs. Harden's return to the house she found her husband had died from gunshots fired by Smith.

"To seek assistance she and the children hurried to a neighbor's home to report the crimes and to get help. Word soon spread through the community of Smith's crimes.

"Several people, including law enforcement officials went to Smith's residence to arrest him for murder. They ordered him to come out of the house and he acknowledged their request and promised to come out. After waiting for a reasonable amount of time, Smith failed to come out, so several people went inside to get him. However, they were surprised to learn that Smith was not there. He had escaped by way of the chimney and they were unable to locate him.

"A discussion centered around where Smith might be hiding. The officers were aware that he had a history of criminal activity. Several months prior to the murder he had broken into a saloon and stole money and a revolver. He had stolen $35.00 from a drunk, and later they learned that on the evening of the murder, he stole a check from an elderly woman who owned a confectionery store.

"Smith could not be located, but the investigation continued. Authorities wasted no time in having an Inquest by Jury, which was conducted by Justice of the Peace Gonder, with J. Browning being the jury foreman.

"The jury found Smith to be responsible for Harden's death, but he was still a fugitive and his whereabouts were unknown by officials.

"On May 19, 1883, four days after the murder, Col. John Veitch, state's attorney for Garrett County, received a dispatch from Winchester, VA, advising that a colored man had been arrested there who answered the description of Smith. However, the person denied being Smith, saying his name was Jackson. In order to establish the identity of Smith/Jackson, the state's attorney asked Jeremiah Browning of Elkins who knew the murderer very well to go to Virginia.

"Upon Browning's arrival in Winchester, he identified the arrested person as Smith. Smith denied knowing Browning and also denied ever being at Elkins.

"Due to the positive identification, the state's attorney requisitioned Smiths return by making application to Governor William Hamilton.

"The murder investigation was continuing, and several days after the murder, several state witnesses were brought before the Justice of the Peace. They included, Mrs. Harden, widow of the murdered man, Robert Harden, son, age 15, Alice Harden, daughter, a Mrs. Lee and two black men who lived in the same house with Smith.

"Justice Gonder required Mrs. Harden and Robert Harden to post $300 bail each or go to jail until the hearing in September. Mrs. Lee was allowed to go home and ordered to appear before the September term of the Grand Jury. The two black men were ordered held on $150 each. Alice Harden, age nine, had no place to stay since her father was dead and her mother and brother were committed to jail in default of bail. Justice Gonder permitted little Alice to stay in jail with her mother and brother.

"On June 5, 1883, the requisition of John Herbert Smith was received by the state's attorney from Governor Hamilton. Sheriff Jamison did not go after Smith for four days because the jail had only one compartment and the sheriff didn't want Smith and the witnesses together. To solve the problem, arrangements were made with the sheriff of Allegany County to accept three witnesses, including Mrs. Harden, Robert Harden, and Mitchell Russell, who lived with Smith.

"The sheriff and state's attorney were quite proud that witness arrangements would not cost the county taxpayers any money. The sheriff of Allegany County received 40 cents per day for boarding a prisoner and the sheriff of Garrett County received 50 cents. As a result, Garrett County would save 10 cents per day per witness, which would more than pay for their transportation to and from Cumberland.

"Enroute to Virginia, the sheriff took the three witnesses to Cumberland, and he went to Richmond where Smith was being held.

"Smith was indicted by the Grand Jury on September 12, 1883, and had a trial by jury beginning on September 18, 1883, and ended on September 21, 1883.

"At the jury trial, Mrs. Harden and her two children gave testimony of events that had occurred on the night of the murder.

"Smith denied the murder charge and he had been busy trying to establish an alibi. He had told Mitchell Russell that he had heard several shots fired at or near the Harden house. That he had heard the children crying and saw two men running away from Harden's house. Mr. Russell also testified that Smith had threatened to kill Harden last spring because Harden had cheated him during a boot transaction. Smith was trying to encourage other black people in the community to lie and say they were at his home on the night of the murder playing cards and dancing, but they refused to lie for him.

"After eluding police on the night of the murder, Smith encouraged other black people to take crowbars and pick handles and beat up those persons who were trying to arrest him, but the black people refused to fight his battles.

"Smith had told a friend that he had killed Harden, and his only regret was that he hadn't killed Mrs. Harden because he felt no one was left who could tell the story.

"In jail, another prisoner had given Smith a knife. He planned to have a successful escape from jail. To assist in the escape, he would cut the sheriff's throat. But a prisoner who was aware of the plans informed the state's attorney, who in turn notified the sheriff. The sheriff disarmed Smith. Smith wanted to escape from jail to avoid trial because he didn't want anyone making a circus out of him in court.

"Smith did not take the witness stand in his own defense, and only two witnesses were called to testify to attempt to disprove some testimony offered by the state.

"The state's attorney, Col. John Veitch, argued before the jury for two and one-half hours for a conviction of first degree murder.

"The two defense attorneys, Mr. H. Wheeler McCombs and Mr. T.J. Peddicord argued for three hours for an acquittal. They were competent trial attorneys and did everything possible for their client. Mr. Peddicord, one of the defense attorneys was a relative of Chief Judge Fred A. Thayer, Circuit Court for Garrett County, Maryland.

"The jury arrived at their verdict in 30 minutes: guilty of first degree murder.

"After the guilty verdict was announced, Smith said, 'The circus is over, next we will have a concert.'

"The sentencing was held on September 24, 1883. Judge Alvey asked Smith if he had anything to say. He said, he did not receive justice and wanted a new trial. If he were guilty he would have confessed it and not gone through a trial.

"If he could have gotten his witnesses it would have been different. But his witnesses were all poor and scattered working on railroads and if they would have been discharged, Smith felt the state witnesses had lied. That he didn't use bad words, that he was neither a thief, robber, nor a cut throat, and it would be no more than right for the court to order a new trial.

"After Smith had taken his seat, Judge Alvey proceeded to deliver the sentence, commented upon the nature, circumstances and enormity of his crime. That Smith had but a short time to live and would soon meet his God. The Judge told Smith to obtain the services of a minister, and urged him to lose no time in preparing for death, then pronounced the death sentence by hanging upon Smith.

"As the sheriff was removing Smith from the court room, he said to the judge, 'You may hang the body but you can't hang the soul. You will be judged yourself some day.' And to the state's attorney he said, 'The devil will get that state's attorney sure and certain.'

"On October 4, 1883, Mr. Smith escaped from the county jail. He had complained of being ill and when the jailer, James Cropp, went into the jail, Smith attacked Mr. Cropp with a bucket, and the jailer stabbed Smith on the breast with a knife during the escape process. Smith was in leg shackles at the time, but after over powering the jailer, Smith escaped and found a hatchet on the back porch of the sheriff's residence, and was able to cut the chain attached to the shackles. The sheriff was downtown, and as soon as he returned, Captain Wardwell of the Garrett Guards was notified of the escape and his unit remained out all night looking for Smith. The next morning, Smith returned to the jail to surrender. He had been stabbed while escaping and he was suffering in pain, and he thought he had been seriously injured.

"Dr. Bartlett examined the wound and found it not to be serious.

"The death warrant fixing the date of the execution was set for Friday, November 16, 1883.

"A lot of planning went into preparing for Smith's execution. "The sheriff sought the legal advise of the attorney general. In a letter from the attorney general dated October 13, 1883, he made the following observations:

"-The sheriff had the authority to command as many male residents of the county as necessary to prevent Smith's escape.

"-The sheriff had the power to protect Smith until he was executed.

"-The sheriff had the power to execute Smith in the county jail if he had the space. If the jail didn't have proper space, he could enclose a yard adjoining the jail, sufficient in size to contain the scaffold and those attending, which is allowed by law, with a strong fence, high enough to exclude the execution from outside view, and to have the fence guarded upon the outside.

"To comply with the advise of the attorney general, Sheriff Jamison had made arrangements for the Garrett Guards to be present, and built a sixteen foot high fence to prevent the public from viewing the execution.

"On the evening prior to the execution, Smith ate a hearty supper and was visited by Rev. Benjamin Ison of the Methodist Church of Oakland.

"Smith talked freely, but felt he was an innocent man. He realized this was his last night on earth and he said he trusted in the Lord, and that he expected to go to heaven. The minister and Smith sang songs. His favorite songs were: *Beulah Land*, *Home Over There*, and *Rock of Ages*.

"The next morning--the day of execution, Smith ate a hearty breakfast, and the Rev. Ison returned for a visit. During the visit, Smith admitted to murdering Mr. Harden. He said that he had nothing against Harden, but blamed liquor for the killing, and he had been encouraged to do it.

"The Garrett Guards, along with 350 people, were present for the execution. Only certain people were allowed to witness the execution, such as, relatives, ministers, sheriff, etc.

"The scaffold was erected by P.A. Chisholm, who had never seen a similar structure. It was well designed and substantially built, and someone remarked that it worked like a charm. The platform was 8' from the ground.

"Smith was given an opportunity to make a statement before his death. He said, 'Farewell to everybody. God bless you all. It's very hard when a man comes to die like this, but it's no difference what the death is, so that the soul is ready to live with God. I am ready to die, I weep, not because I am to die, but because of the deed for which I am accused. I don't deny it. I done it. I, John Herbert Smith. But, I was persuaded to do it, and was under the influence of liquor at the time. I have prayed to God to forgive me and hope my fellow man have forgiven me.' Then he said to the sheriff, 'I am ready.' Again, he said, 'Goodbye and God bless you.' He expressed hope that someone would take care of his wife. It was later determined that he wasn't married, just living in a common law relationship.

"Smith observed a man in front of him sobbing. He said, 'Don't weep, my friend, it's all for the better.'

"Mr. Smith requested that one of his attorneys, McCombs be present during the execution. The other attorney, Mr. Peddicord, was a member of the Garrett Guards and was assigned outside the jail to assist in making certain that Smith did not escape.

"After the execution, Smith was buried nearby.

"This ends the case of the State of Maryland vs. John Herbert Smith, Garrett County's first murderer.

Wayne Wilt
November, 1989"

Murder occurred May 15, 1883.
Apprehended in Winchester May 19, 1883.
Requisition from Governor Hamilton June 5, 1883.
Sheriff goes to Richmond for Smith June 9, 1883.
Witnesses to Allegany Co. jail June 9, 1883.
Trial by jury Sept. 18, 1883.
Trial ended (guilty) Sept. 21, 1883.
Sentencing Sept. 24, 1883.
Escape from jail Oct. 4, 1883.
Surrendered October 5, 1883.
Letter to sheriff from attorney general Oct. 13, 1883.
Execution Nov. 16, 1883.
From crime to execution-six months.

"To the Sheriff of Garrett County

"Whereas John Smith colored was convicted in the Circuit Court of Garrett County at September term in the year one thousand eight hundred and eighty three of murder in the first degree. And whereas the said court sentenced him to be hung by the neck until he be dead.

"Now therefore these are to will and require, as also to charge and command you, that, at or before the hour of two o'clock pm on Friday the sixteenth day of November next, you take the said John Smith, colored from your prison, and him safely convey to the gallows in the County aforesaid, the place of the execution of malefactors, and then and there the said John Smith, colored hang by the neck until he be dead. For all which this shall be your sufficient power and authority.

"Given under my hand and the Great Seal of the State of Maryland, at the city of Annapolis on the fourth day of October, in the year of our Lord eighteen hundred and eighty three, and of the Independence of the United States the one hundred and seventh.

"By the Governor; William Hamilton
Secretary of State: James Briscoe"

"I, Edmund Jamison late Sheriff of Garrett County hereby certify that under and by virtue of the power and authority vested in me by the written warrant and in obedience to the command therein I did on the 16th day of November in the year 1883 take the within John Smith from the jail of said County and did in the jail yard execute upon him the death sentence as in said warrant commanded at the hour of one o'clock and fourteen minutes p.m. of said day as will appear by physicians certificates hereto annexed.

Edmund Jamison, Late Sheriff"

All information and statements were copied from the official records on file at the Oakland Courthouse.

"Oakland, Garrett Co. Md.
November 16, 1883
On the 16th of November 1883 at the request of the Sheriff of
Garrett Co., I was present at the hanging for the murder of
Josiah Harden. I hereby certify that the execution in all its de-
tails was properly conducted. The hanging at 1:14 o'clock pm
and death taking place in twelve minutes. The body was al-
lowed to hang for some minutes after death, and was taken down
at 1:45, or thirty one minutes after the drop.
E.H. Bartlett, M.D."

"Oakland, Maryland
November 19, 1883
I, J. Lee McComas M.D. Physician for the jail in and for
Garrett Co. Md., appointed as such by the Commissioners of
said County, hereby certify that Edmund Jamison, Sheriff in
and for said County and State did take from the Jail of said
Garrett County one John Herbert Smith, (who was tried and
found guilty of murder, and was sentenced by the Court sitting
in and for said County at the September term 1883 to be hung
by the neck until dead) and did execute said sentence on the
sixteenth day of November 1883 at one o'clock and thirteen
minutes p.m. and that said John Herbert Smith was then and
there hanged by the neck until he was dead.
J. Lee McComas, M.D.
Jail Physician"

Historical Interest

The hanging took place on what is now the Board of Education property, and the body was buried there. When the last
addition to the High School was built, part of the skeleton of
John Smith was found, as workers were excavating for the foun-
dation.

The local undertaker, Mr. Emroy Rolden, was notified. He
came and picked out the bones and placed them in a standard-
size "rough box". It was then taken to the Oakland Cemetery
and re-buried; the location unknown.

Elkins was the name for Gorman. On Monday, December 17, 1888, the names for several of the stations on the West Virginia Central Railroad were changed as follows: "Gorman will be called Steyer, Elkins will be called Gorman, and Leadsville will be called Elkins."

The Harden family had three members who died violent deaths: Josiah from being shot, Michael was killed by a train, and William was killed by a train.

"Killed At Frostburg.
Michael Harden, Former Accident Resident Met With Fatal Accident.

"While driving across the tracks of the Western Maryland Railway near the Borden Mining Company's farm, a short distance above Frostburg, at noon on Tuesday, Michael Harden, employed as a farm hand on the farm of James Engle, his son-in-law, was ground to pieces and his two horses were instantly killed when struck by passenger train No. 2 on its way east from Pittsburgh. John Sullivan, who was walking in the rear of the wagon, escaped injury. The train as a result of the accident was delayed an hour.

"For many years Mr. Harden, prior to moving to Frostburg, resided at Accident and was employed as star route carrier between Oakland and his home town. He was a brother-in-law of the Messrs. Shartzer of Oakland.

"The body of Mr. Harden was taken to Frostburg where it was later removed for burial near Frostburg. Mr. Harden is survived by his wife, Mrs. Barbara Harden and the following sons and daughters: Mrs. James Engle, Mrs. W. Blocher, Mrs. Harry Kellar, Samuel Harden, Edward Harden, all of Frostburg; Mrs. James Harden of Eckhart and Mrs. McGuire of Grantsville.

"The funeral occurred at Frostburg yesterday afternoon at four o'clock."

Fatal Accident

"A sad accident occurred near Swanton on the B&O railroad on last Saturday night, November 9, 1889, in which William Harden, of Accident, lost his life, and the news of which, when brought to Accident on Sabbath afternoon, caused the hearts of his parents and near relatives to overflow with grief and sorrow.

"Just exactly how it happened no one knows. The following particulars however were furnished the writer and are as near correct as can at present be known. Mr. Harden, it seems, had bought a ticket to Piedmont and return, and had gone to Piedmont. It is supposed that he missed the westward bound mail train, and then either walked part of the way or boarded a freight train and rode to No. 40 and got off there, and then got on again, or else waited till the train from which he was thrown came along and stopped at No. 40 to take in water and then boarded it, as he was seen by some of the train men at some little distance ahead of the standing train approaching it. About a quarter of a mile from No. 40 (a water tank below Swanton) it is supposed the accident occurred. His watch was found first, then his hat, vest and coat. His body was carried to the crossing at Swanton where it was dropped, and was found between 9 and 10 o'clock by Jno. Uphold and Pat Coyle, considerably mangled. His head was cut off from the right ear down to the neck at the left shoulder. His face and skull were all crushed. His legs were broken as well as one arm. The mangled body was brought to Accident on Sunday afternoon by Mr. Bolden of Oakland.

"On Monday at 10 o'clock services were held in the English Lutheran Church at Accident. The sermon was preached from 2 Samuel, 18th chapter 33rd verse. A large audience was present and a large concourse of people followed the remains to the grave. His remains were laid in the English Lutheran cemetery. He was 26 years and 29 days old. "Billy" as he was familiarly called, carried the mail for a number of years from Accident to Grantsville. At the time of his death, he was carrying the mail from Oakland to Accident."

Harden Family

James Harden, (May 20, 1812 in PA. - Jan. 27, 1891)
at 4 am in Accident, MD
Married on January 30, 1838 to
Rebecca Porter   (Aug. 9, 1820 - April 30, 1906)
dau. of Michael and Elizabeth (DeVore) Porter
Children:

Josiah,   (March 24, 1839 - May 15, 1883) (murdered by John Smith) married on Jan. 20, 1862 to Harriet E. Martin

Emmaline,   (Jan. 15, 1842 - June 13, 1928) married Nov. 8, 1860 to Valentine Kahl (May 27, 1838 - April 11, 1925)

Michael Edward, (April 5, 1844 - July 11, 1916) married Barbara Shartzer. Michael was killed by a train, just out of Frostburg at Borden.

Elizabeth,   (April 4, 1845 -   )

Nancy Ellen,   (June 26, 1846 - July 14, 1862) died at the age of sixteen years old

Mary,   (January 1, 1852 -   )

Martin,   (March 12, 1855 -   )

George,   (April 30, 1857 -   )

Harriet,   (April 1, 1859 - May 14, 1940) married on June 13, 1875 to Samuel Pritts, he died Nov. 3, 1924 in Akron, Ohio.

William,   (Oct. 11, 1861 - Nov. 9, 1889) William was killed by a train at Swanton, MD.

Ralph D.   (May 26, 1862 -   )

Ida Florence,   (Dec. 14, 1863 -   )

James Walter,   (Jan. 21, 1866 -   )

Samuel K.   (Jan. 28, 1867 -   )

The marriage license for James Harden and Rebecca Porter is on file at the Allegany County Courthouse, Cumberland, Maryland as is the marriage license for the first three children.

Josiah Harden Family

Josiah Harden, (March 24, 1839 - May 15, 1883)
married on January 20, 1862 to
Harriet E. Martin,
Children:
James Harden,
Robert Harden, (b. about 1868 -   )
Rebbeca Harden,
Married Sam Lewis
Ida Harden, (b. 1873 -
married on Sept. 4, 1895 to
William J. Bowermaster (b. 1873 -
Alice Mae Harden,
(May 14, 1874 - March 31, 1960 in Ohio)
married on Feb. 23, 1895 to
Henry Shearer Kling (Mar. 30, 1865 -
Mar. 14, 1915)

She Chopped Off His Head

"James Male, married Susan Murphy, and they lived for years on a small farm not far from Altamont. Here they raised a family of sons and daughters, among them John, Lewis, Harriet and Ells. James, according to the story vouched for by one of his nephews, got drunk one cold winter day and threatened to kill his wife. She managed to avoid him, and took the children out to a haystack, where she hid them for protection from the cold. She then got the axe with which she was accustomed to cut firewood and sneaked up to the house. Her husband by that time was dozing in a drunken stupor in a corner. One version has it that one of the boys shot at the father with a rifle, but missed. Be that as it may, Susan crept up to the sleeping man and chopped off his head. It is said that she then went to Cumberland, the county seat (Garrett County then being part of Allegany County,) and related to the authorities what had taken place. So far as is known, no action ever was taken against her, for search of the court records of Allegany County for that period reveals no mention of the incident whatever. Susan lived quietly thereafter on the farm with her family. She acquired quite a reputation locally as a "Yarb Doctor," and often was called in case of sickness or accident when "Old" Doctor McComas was not available. One instance is recalled when she cured what was said to be a case of dropsy by the application of a piece of sod heated in the oven of the kitchen stove. She died in 1884 and is buried in an unmarked grave under a tamarack tree in the Deer Park cemetery. James is said to have been buried in a fence corner on the farm."

Tintype of Susan Male, herb doctor and midwife of many years ago when doctors were few and far between. She killed her husband, Jim Male, with an axe, when he attacked her with a butcher knife in their cabin on the Hardesty farm near Deer Park, before the Civil War.

The Murder of Abraham Frey

"We are indebted to the Garrett County historian, Felix Robinson, and to that Western Maryland classic, Lowdermilk's History of Cumberland, for the following account of a crime which took place many years ago in the vicinity of Selbysport, then in Allegany but since 1872 included within the boundaries of Garrett County:

"On July 22, 1843, Abraham Frey, living near Selbysport, was murdered by William S. Chrise, a short distance from Frey's house. Chrise was a large, rugged man, and for some time had been on undue terms of intimacy with Mrs. Frey. This had led to the husband's forbidding Chrise to come to his home. Chrise resented this and threatened to kill Frey and take the latter's wife for himself. On one occasion, indeed, he did attempt to abduct her. On the 22nd of July Chrise met Frey in the woods near the latter's home and struck him with a heavy hoe, the blow falling on the back of his head and crushing the victim's skull.

"The murderer then concealed the body of his victim behind a fallen tree where it was found some days later. Chrise then was arrested and brought to Cumberland, the county seat, where he was confined in jail until October 16th when his trial took place. On October 17th a jury was obtained. Messrs. Hanson B. Pigman and William V. Buskirk were counsel for the prosecution. George A. Pearre, who was to become a well known figure in Cumberland in later years, and who then was a young lawyer at the bar, was counsel for the defense. At Mr. Pearre's request the Court appointed William Price as additional counsel for the prisoner. The trial was concluded on the fourth day, and in twenty minutes the jury returned a verdict of 'Guilty of murder in the first degree.' Sentence was passed by the Court on October 20th. It was, as might have been expected under the circumstances, that the defendant be hanged by the neck until dead.

"The execution of Chrise took place in November. The prisoner was utterly unmoved throughout the trying ordeal, and apparently was the least interested of all the great crowd assembled on the occasion. He walked from the jail to the scaffold which had been erected on the commons, at a point near the Fayette Street crossing of the Baltimore and Ohio Railroad. On the route to the scaffold the prisoner was guarded by 'The Cumberland Guards,' commanded by Alexander King, with a drum and fife in advance. The services at the place of execution were quite lengthy and impressive, several hymns being sung, in all of which the prisoner joined. During the intervals Chrise sat calmly chewing tobacco, occasionally rising from his seat to spit beyond the fatal trap, as though fearing to soil it. Just before the last moment he sang in a clear, loud and unbroken voice, a hymn of which the following couplet is a part: 'This is the way I long have sought And mourned because I found it not.'

"The Sheriff, Norman Bruce, was deeply affected by the unpleasant duty he was called on to perform, and it was doubtless the most painful act in his life. When the rope was cut several witnesses of the scene fainted, and much excitement prevailed. Amongst those who looked on was a brother of the doomed man who seemed to be little affected, but remarked– 'It is a pretty hard sight.' When life became extinct the body was taken down and conveyed to the old Court House where the physicians made some experiments with it. It afterwards was dissected, and old Joe Shumate, an eccentric man, and regarded as very wicked, secured a portion of the dead man's skin and tanned it, the leather proving soft and pliable."

The Ghost of "Spook Hollow"

By R. Getty Browning

"Many years ago when Meshach Browning and his family lived at Sang Run, a frolic or party was to be held at one of the neighbor's homes near Accident, and among those invited were William Browning, John L. Browning and their sister, Jane. It was intended that the young people would stay all night after the party and that the next day the boys would go hunting, consequently William took his rifle along. They left their home late in the afternoon, William riding one horse, Jane another and John L. walking, the arrangement being that the boys would ride turn about, and the one who rode would carry the rifle, as they were not expecting to see any game along the road. Their path led across 'Spook Hollow,' a place situated near their home, and where a number of strange things had been seen by various persons. Up to that time the Brownings had never seen any-

thing out of the ordinary at this place or anywhere else for that matter, and they were not people to be unduly excited by any strange event.

"William and John L., sons of Meshach Browning, the famous hunter, had participated with him in many bear fights, and were noted for their coolness, courage and levelheadness; therefore, it is all the more singular that they, on this occasion, saw something which they never clearly understood. They reached 'Spook Hollow' a little after sundown, and it was John L.'s turn to walk. He was perhaps 20 yards ahead of the horses when he suddenly saw some horrible monster standing a few feet off the trail. He never saw anything like it before, and as he described it, it appeared to be about the size of a yearling bear, which would be as tall as a good size collie but much heavier. This beast, however, appeared to be devoid of hair, having a skin like an elephant or a toad, and instead of having a head such as a bear or any other animal known to them, it seemed to have a human face set right into the base of its neck or rather directly in the shoulders. It was standing on a small hickory pole which had fallen; it made no move to advance or retreat, and it made no sound. John L. had seen many a wild cat, panther and bear, but here was something entirely different. He called to William, 'Bring the gun, Bill, here's the devil and I want to shoot him.' William and Jane rode up beside John L. and they too had a good look at the beast; although John L. insisted that William give him the gun so that he could shoot it, William thought that it was such an unusual creature that it was better not to molest it. Therefore, he told John L. to come along and not bother it. This could not possibly have been a matter of imagination since they all saw it; the horses did too, because as long as those horses were used on that trail, they recognized this spot and showed signs of nervousness and fright whenever they passed it.

"The question is: 'What was this apparition?' The writer when quite young had an opportunity to talk to John L. about this occurrence; he stated that he felt sure that it was the devil that they saw. He described the appearance of the animal just as I have given it. William, however, evidently thought that whatever they saw, it was beyond anything in nature and he did not like to talk about it too much, although he corroborated the description given above.

"*Spook Hollow is on the John F. Friend farm at Sang Run. The entrance to 'Old' John Friend's Salt Petre Cave is nearby."

John Friend Cave

"The matter of exploring caves is known as 'spelunking.' The entrance to one of the few caves in Garrett County is hidden in a grove of oaks on the Friend farm at Sang Run. The cave's rightful and legal name is the 'John Friend Saltpetre Cave,' as mentioned in Col. Francis Deakin's survey of military lots in 1787. Although the cave has the connotation 'salt-petre' there is little evidence that it was used extensively for salt petre earth. The only evidence of digging is in the rear portion where a large stalagmite has been all but obliterated by chipping. The Cave itself is entirely a natural formation, carved out of limestone by a stream that flows over its floor.

"John Friend Cave has been known since colonial days. Ample proof that the cave was explored at an early date are names dating back to the seventeen hundreds. G.S. Hamill and J.C. Willison were there in 1925; John T. Browning was there in 1866; Mary Hinebaugh added hers in 1776.

"Another room, a small junction of passages, seems to invite the autographs of many who have visited the cave, for its walls are literally covered with names, F.C. Stahl, D.E. Bolden, Linn and John Grant, E. Custer, July 3, 1880, Della Savage, October 17, 1894, E.A. Browning, May 1, 1871, Mr. and Mrs. C.W. Kemp, October 2, 1872, Isaac Saxon, 1870, Berlin and E.C. Woodrup, 1809, are a few of the host of monikers scratched in the mud.

"The cave has been closed for many years because cattle and horses often fell in and either broke legs or got lost." (*From a 1948 article*)

Dead Man Cave

According to local residents this used to be a rather extensive and frequently visited cave in the 19th century. The cave takes its name from a legend connected with its history. The legend has it that a family named Sines, in which there were two brothers, lived in the area in the 1860s. One of them was reportedly retarded and was murdered by the other, who buried his body in the cave which was subsequently filled up. In the 1960s a spelunker undertook to re-open the cave. A trash-filled sink was entered and about 150 feet of passage explored to the site of an extensive blockage of fallen rock, which could not be bypassed. This particular sinkhole was revisited in 1970, and found to be closed at the bottom by an earth slump.

Braddock's Gold

by Ross C. Durst

"Many years ago, I spent most of my vacation tramping over the old Braddock Trail. I was attempting to relocate the old road-bed. While U.S. 40 follows the general route of Braddock's road, yet in only a few spots does it follow it exactly. In spots they are several miles apart. It was while I was engaged in this task that I began hearing the stories about Braddock's gold.

"It is a well known fact that Braddock carried a considerable supply of gold to pay his men and to pay for supplies. The story

Braddock's Grave

has always persisted that after his defeat, this chest, variously estimated to contain from $5,000 to $125,000, was buried somewhere on the retreat to Fort Cumberland.

"Considerably more than a century ago, a traveler on the road west of Cumberland met an old grey-haired man carrying a crowbar and searching along a stream bed. He told the traveler that his father had been one of six men whose duty it was to guard the chest of gold and get it safely back to the fort after the rout began. According to his story, their party was ambushed by Indians, three of the party being killed instantly and his father was injured. The two uninjured guards left the chest in his care and pushed on toward the fort. They were never seen again, presumably having been killed. The chest had been carefully secreted in a small cave along a streambed.

"Some days later when a body of soldiers arrived, his father was found wandering along Braddock Run near Wills Creek, delirious from his wounds. He was unable to tell anyone where the chest had been hidden. After his recovery, he tried unsuccessfully to find the gold. After peace came, he married and built a cabin in the mountain. For the rest of his life, he devoted all his spare time to the search. After his death, the search was continued by the son with the same discouraging results.

"Many years ago there stood a large oak tree on the side of the old Braddock Road just where it crossed the county road to Avilton, MD. On one large branch overhanging the road, the leaves would turn yellow early in the summer while the rest of the tree remained green. The story was circulated, and believed, that this was nature's way of indicating the location of the lost gold. Every summer would find some party industriously digging in the hard rocky soil beneath the tree. Eventually, the tree died, perhaps as a result of the excavations. At any rate, no gold was found and the story subsided."

Castle Hill

by Francis Turner

"The 'Castle Hill' land tract, 50 acres, was surveyed in 1774 for Gen. John Swan and patented to him in 1790. It was located on the old Glades Path near the summit of Backbone Mountain, and was doubtless a camping place of Indians, hunters, herders and early settlers, and later the site of a noted inn on the old State Road.

"The name 'Castle Hill', was probably suggested to General Swan, or to his surveyor, by the appearance of the mountain at that point. Looking north east from the old tavern site this ridge of Backbone resembles the broken-down walls or battlements of some giant's castle.

"James Stackpole kept an inn or tavern at Castle Hill very early. Thomas Walcut mentions his place in writing of a trip over the State Road in 1790. Prior to 1800 Stackpole moved to Doddridge County, Virginia, where his descendants still live. Robert Abernathy and others kept the tavern until 1852, when part of the log inn was torn down and the rest used as a farm house. In 1886 the Henry G. Davis saw mill was moved from the head of Elk Lick Run; the frame boarding house was moved to Castle Hill and rebuilt into the present house at the spring, near the old tavern site."

Mysterious Graves of Castle Hill

"A group of neighbors were gathered one Sunday to see the new house. They talked of the history of the place, and of the old graves on the roadside nearby. Some one said that he had heard that four of Gen. Braddock's soldiers, part of a party fleeing from the defeat of the army in 1755, died at Castle Hill and were buried there. But old Col. Wm. McCrobie said that in his boyhood days he had heard the old people of the neighborhood say that the graves were of Virginia Militia, part of a party returning to their homes from General Forbes' army after the capture of Fort Duquesne in 1758.

"Some one opened one of the graves and found only bones and some rusty hand forged nails. It is said that soldiers were buried in split logs, hollowed out to serve as coffins, the ends closed with puncheons, spiked on with big nails.

"Such are the stories of the graves on Castle Hill, all of which indicate that this was a very old camping place and settlement, its history almost lost.

"Ned Robbird's (Robert's?) Cabin stood, long ago, on the North side of the State Road just east of the Castle Hill place. In the Survey's of 'Castle Hill' and of Military Lot 100 Robbird's cabin is mentioned in locating a corner.

"Ned's tragic story, as told by Rezin Turner and others, is that after he and his wife built their cabin, a man named Davis from down the river came to visit them. One day he offered to chop wood for the fire place and asked Ned to show him the wood to be cut. While they were away from the cabin Davis killed Ned with the ax, and buried him in a shallow grave by the cabin. He then took Ned's wife to his hunting camp on the Potomac.

"It was said that Ned's uneasy spirit long returned at night to his cabin and grave; people of the neighborhood, until last generation, used to shun the place, and they still point out the site of Ned's cabin."

Robbery of the Swanton Post Office

The Swanton Post Office was the scene of a robbery, as told in the November 1911 issue of *The Republican* newspaper. This robbery occurred 14 years prior to the robbery of 1925. This article is taken from the paper's account of the 1911 robbery.

"Prominent among the more recent of Swanton's public buildings is a new post office, fresh from the architect's hands, hugging the south side of Merchant Good's more pretentious building and with that building facing the railroad platform.

"This newly finished office was a neat little structure of two rooms, generously answering all the requirements of the office,

with the public in one apartment and the United States officials conducting the affairs of the Government in the other division. Merchant Good with Mrs. Good occupied rooms over the store. These rooms are reached by two long flights of stairways, one from the front and one from the rear.

"About two o'clock on the morning of November 2nd, 1911, the merchant was aroused by a jarring crash which he first thought might be from the slam of a door by the postmaster, Mr. Albert Baker, arranging the early mail; discovering that it was only two o'clock, he went to a window and could distinctly hear the rambling of thieves in the postoffice, but too close under the side of the store to be seen from the window. He had at command only a small revolver and with it fired through the open window down in the direction of the working robbers. An answering fire quickly came from the outside, the ball crashing in destruction through three large glass panels of the window of the store directly beneath Mr. Good. With criminal daring the villains proceeded heedless, apparently, of the ordinary caution of stealth. Soon Mr. Good repeated his fire, drawing again a quick response fire, it seemed at random. In a short time stillness prevailed, the robbery had been accomplished and under the curtain of night the demons slunk away unseen.

"The rascally intention was deliberately planned. Buckets and similar obstructions had been placed along the steps of the two mentioned stairways to trip any one who might run down the steps in the dark.

"When Mr. Baker arrived at his usual hour, the office was in ruins. The intruders forced an entrance through a back window, then going forward to the public part where a strong iron safe stood. By an explosive, many times more powerful than was needed for their accomplishment, they demolished the safe, blowing parts into fragments and twisting other parts in intricate shapes. The violence of the explosion not only shattered the glass in all the windows, but tore a large hole in the planks of the floor and left the partition in a serpentine appearance with many breaks.

By a fortunate chance only a small amount of change had been left the previous evening in the safe, but the equal of $117 or more was there in stamps and other valuables taken in the haul."

Swanton Post Office, 1925, Joseph F. Friend, P.M.

Gun Battle at Swanton Post Office-1925

Joseph Fletcher Friend, II
(1869-1930)

"Our story tells of sudden and deadly violence during a gun battle in darkness on an autumn night in the lonely mountains of western Maryland. It was fought between a then unknown bandit and a brave man protecting the United States Mail in defense of his life. The bandit had broken into the combination country store-post office building beside the B.&O. railroad tracks in the village of Swanton, Garrett County.

"The defender was Postmaster Joseph Fletcher Friend II, age 56, who everyone called 'Joe'.

27

The bandit was later identified as Henderson Hall, a negro from Jamaica and classed as a 'Wanted man' by Baltimore police two hundred miles to the east.

"The bandit had a white accomplice, Ralph Anderson, a young man who lived with his parents in a poor shack near the top of Backbone Mountain that overlooks Swanton village. Hall had somehow made Anderson's acquaintance and they had been seen riding freight trains on the afternoon of September 17, 1925, and had passed through Swanton several times. After the event we will describe, it was learned that the two had stopped on that day at a Wilt family home near Bond and asked for food which they were given. They were ready to rob the Swanton Post Office and went to the building about 10 P.M. that night where Anderson was posted outside as lookout while Hall forced an entrance.

"Postmaster Friend did not see Ralph Anderson on the night of the attempted robbery, but he knew him and had helped the man's family by furnishing food at different times to them. He also knew that Ralph Anderson was not of strong character and did not try to find work. The Anderson family were newcomers to the community.

"Postmaster Friend had a family. One of the sons, Lawton, was working in Philadelphia. Charles, another son, was a Western Union lineman who serviced the communication lines along the railroad and was stationed in Grafton. The Friend home was just across the tracks in the village within shouting distance of the place where Mr. Friend worked. But Joe Friend took his responsibility to heart and guarded the U.S. Mail and the store contents by sleeping in a room adjoining the main room used for merchandise and the post office area that was partitioned from the public. He was asleep there on that September night. And on the night stand beside his bed, the postmaster kept a loaded .38 caliber revolver and a flashlight. He had come to manhood accustomed to guns and hunting.

"Railroaders and those who live beside a busy mainline, know the tremendous noise made by great mallet steam engines and passenger trains roaring under full throttle up mountain grades. They are conditioned to sleep to the accompaniment of train whistles blowing for road crossings as they did then, and diesels still do, at Swanton on the famous Seventeen-Mile grade of the B.&O. east-west line. And Joe Friend slept that night in 1925 within twenty feet of passing engines and trains.

"A noise strange to his surroundings awakened the postmaster. He heard the sound again, just beyond his bedroom door; knew that someone was moving in the Post Office area of the large store room. He got up and stood barefooted in his long underwear. He was a big man, a six-footer, weighing about 185 pounds. He lifted his gun and flashlight from the table. Joe moved toward the door in the darkness and fear was not part of his feelings. He opened the door and flicked on his light.

"Death flashed at him with the roar of a gunshot and missed Joe by only a hair. A terrific blow struck the left side of his head. He staggered against the door jamb but did not go down. He fired at the other's gunflash and dropped his flashlight. He heard a gasping grunt and a body slam against the partition in the Post Office. Hot blood poured down the side of Joe's face. He surged forward and leaped over the store counter. Now he faced the small window of the Post Office wall. The bandit shot again and Friend's gun blasted in answer. Joe rushed to the small window and began firing into the mail storage area.

"Another bullet from the bandit's pistol slashed across the top of Joe's head, tearing a bloody gash through his scalp. His revolver snapped on an empty shell and Joe dropped his gun. He now realized his enemy had stopped shooting. He plunged through the Post Office door and grappled with the other man. Joe's hands slipped on his enemy's blood-smeared throat and they went to the floor as Joe hung on. But his assailant beat the postmaster in the face with the butt of his empty pistol. Joe suffered this shock with the realization he could not overpower the other man. He stopped struggling and pretended to be unconscious and dying. The bandit wrenched himself upright and stumbled out of the building.

"Gasping for breath and in awful pain, Joe Friend managed to get up and get to the outside door and fresh air. He began to scream for help. It came almost at once. As a man ran over the crossing, calling the postmaster's name, Joe knew that his friend and B.&O. agent, Wade H. Lohr, had come to his rescue. Mr. Lohr led the injured man toward his home. They heard nothing of the man who had so seriously wounded the postmaster.

"Mr. Friend's family met him at the low bridge over Crabtree creek and Burzzie Wilt was with Mrs. Estella Friend and the daughters. Burzzie Wilt boarded with the Friend family and carried mail on Route 3 into the Dry Run community. Agent Lohr told the others he would go to the railroad telephone and call the sheriff in Oakland. Swanton is twelve miles east of Oakland.

"The gunfire had awakened Olive Friend. She heard a man yelling. She shook Pearl, Mrs. Campbell, awake, saying, 'Pearl, wake up! I think I hear Dad screaming!' Then Olive ran to get her mother aroused and to awaken their boarder. Mrs. Campbell now remembers that she was barefooted and could not keep up with the others as they hurried toward the Post Office.

"Mr. Lohr's message reached Sheriff Guy Yutzy in Oakland. The night trick telegraphers in the railroad towers were also alerted. Within less than an hour, Sheriff Yutzy arrived by automobile with deputy William Casteel and Dr. N.I. Broadwater, Oakland physician, was with them. Neighbors were already at the Friend home. Men soon came from as far away as Oakland. They were armed, for the news had suggested that more than one bandit was trying to kill people around Swanton.

"While Dr. Broadwater examined Joe Friend, the postmaster told the sheriff that he was sure at least one of his shots had found its mark. The officers went immediately to search for the gunman.

"Dr. Broadwater saw at once that Joe Friend must be hospitalized. He instructed Agent Lohr to request the railroad dispatcher to stop eastbound passenger Train No. 2 at Swanton and pick up Mr. Friend. The doctor gave the wounded man medicine to ease his suffering and dressed the ruined eye and the bloody gash in his scalp. He knew that either wound could have brought instant death if it had varied slightly. He found that the pistol clubbing had broken the lower jawbone and suspected Joe's upper face bones were fractured also.

"Mrs. Campbell remembers that only a short time passed until they heard the sheriff's car come over the railroad crossing and stop before their home. They went outside and found he had captured the bandit whom they now knew to be a negro of powerful physique. She recalls that the man's features were rough and that he did not speak a word when shaken and commanded to answer the sheriff's questions. She says that Dr.

Broadwater examined the prisoner.

"The physician found that the negro had been shot in the groin and Joe Friend said he was convinced this happened with his first shot. The doctor then stated that the prisoner had been shot in the head. He found no evidence that the steel jacketed bullet had come out. The sheriff and his deputy then started for Oakland with the negro. No one knew who he was.

"Preparations had now been completed for taking Mr. Friend to the hospital in Cumberland. Friends made sure that he and Mrs. Friend were put safely aboard Train No. 2 and they left Swanton around midnight.

"Mrs. Campbell remembers that most of the people returned to their homes after the train left. But she says that perhaps as many as ten men stayed at their house to guard herself and Olive. They laid their revolvers and pistols on the dining room table but stayed within reach of these weapons. The sheriff had recovered the bandit's weapon which was a German Luger pistol. The Friends had it for several years.

"Deciding that his prisoner was critically wounded and knowing that he had committed a Federal crime, Sheriff Yutzy transferred the negro to Cumberland. Hospitalized and under Federal custody, the bandit's wounds were treated by the hospital physician who found just how effective Joe Friend's marksmanship had been. The postmaster's bullet had ripped through Hall's face into his skull where it lodged near the base of the brain. The gunshot wound in the groin was serious. But Hall did not die.

"An account published in The *Republican* newspaper at Oakland on September 24, 1925, stated that the 'bullet which is still in his (Hall's) head close to the base of his skull has almost completely paralyzed him.' The late Dennis T. Rasche noted that Hall was kept in the Cumberland hospital for about a month and then moved to the Allegany County jail. Mr. Rasche cited newspaper statements that Hall remained in the jail as a helpless imbecile. The prisoner was never brought to trial because of his physical and mental condition.

"Ralph Anderson, Hall's white accomplice, had fled the scene at the Post Office when the gunfire erupted. He was captured on the Saturday following the Thursday occurrence of the crime by deputy sheriff William Casteel and B.&O. police sergeant

E.W. Athey. They had found him hiding out in the mountain area near his home. He was lodged briefly in the Oakland jail before he, too, was taken to Cumberland and released to Federal authorities. From Mr. Rasche's account we learn that 'Anderson at first denied having any part in the affair. Later, in February 1926, he pleaded guilty to having helped to plan the robbery and to having acted as lookout'. When Anderson appeared before U.S. Commissioner Thomas J. Anderson (no relation), in Cumberland, his bail was set at $4,000. Unable to post bail, Ralph Anderson was remanded to the Allegany County jail to await action of a Federal grand jury.

"Postmaster Friend suffered the loss and removal of his left eye at the Western Maryland Hospital on September 27, 1925. He later traveled to Baltimore for the intended trial of his assailant which did not take place. He returned home but never regained his former health. He died about five years after his desperate struggle with Hall. Three long years after the savage encounter at Swanton, the following entry was published in the Congressional Record, page 1859, Chapter 699, H.R. (Private No. 170)–An Act For the relief of Joseph F. Friend, Payment to: "Be it enacted by the Senate and House of Representatives of the United States of America in Congress assembled, That the Secretary of the Treasury be, and he is hereby authorized and directed to pay, out of any money in the Treasury not otherwise appropriated, and in full settlement against the Government, the sum of $2,000 to Joseph F. Friend, of Swanton, Maryland, for the capture and arrest of Henderson Hall, a negro who attempted the robbery of the post office at Swanton, Maryland. Approved May 22, 1928."

"This was small recompense for the suffering and disability that Postmaster Friend sustained in his struggle to protect the U.S. Mail, defend his life, and uphold the honor of his name and Government position. But this was Joseph Fletcher Friend's creed as it had been that of his father, Civil War veteran, Sergeant Joseph Fletcher Friend I, who served his country with honor in Co. K, 3rd Maryland Regiment, Potomac Home Brigade. Now, father and son rest together in the George Cemetery near Swanton."

"Note: The editor appreciates the privilege of revising research material provided for the story of Joseph F. Friend. The *Glades*

Star's ability to publish the material came from personal knowledge and interviews offered by Mr. Friend's daughters, Mrs. Leroy Campbell and Mrs. Howard P. Lowman, of Swanton; the late *Glades Star* editor, Mr. Dennis T. Rasche; Mr. William Casteel, of Oakland; *Glades Star* associate editor Mr. Paul T. Calderwood and Mrs. Calderwood; the files of The *Republican* newspaper, and from the Congressional excerpt by Congressman Goodloe Byron's office in Washington, DC.

Anderson Pleads Guilty to Post Office Robbery

"When the case of Ralph Anderson, aged 26, of Swanton, was called for trial in the United States Court for the District of Maryland at Baltimore on Monday, the traverser entered a plea of guilty before Judge Morris A. Soper, who was presiding, to being an accessory in the attempt made about three months ago to rob the post office at Swanton, sixteen miles east of Oakland, on the Seventeen-mile grade. Anderson was placed under arrest as a suspect by Harry D. Schmidt, chief of police of the Baltimore and Ohio Railroad, to whom he later made a confession of his part in the attempted robbery of the office.

"Sheriff Guy O. Yutzy, of Garrett County, assisted by Deputy Sheriff W.D. Casteel, of Oakland, arrested Henderson Hall, colored, the morning following the attempt to rob the office. Hall had been badly wounded by Postmaster Joseph F. Friend, when he was found in the office by the postmaster. Hall escaped from the building, however, and was found lying along the railway tracks some distance from the scene. He was brought to the Oakland jail and the following morning was taken into a Cumberland hospital where he was treated for his injuries for some time and then removed as a Federal prisoner to the Cumberland jail where he still remains. It is said that he has been paralyzed as a result of the wound he received, the bullet from Mr. Friend's revolver entering his eye and piercing his brain.

"Mr. Friend, in the battle following Hall's discovery in the act of robbing the post office also received a wound from a bullet fired by Hall, which entered his face and destroyed the sight of

33

one eye.

"Anderson lived with his parents in a cabin located some distance up on the mountain from Swanton and in his alleged confession to the Baltimore and Ohio officer, declared that he met Hall on the day preceding the attempted robbery and that they both plotted to loot the post office. Anderson said he acted as 'lookout' by remaining on watch on the outside of the building while Hall climbed thru a window to do the robbing.

"It is only problematical when Hall will be tried. The condition of the man is said to be such that he is unable to express his desires, hence he cannot be brought into court and tried on the charge standing against him. What disposition to make of the man is a source of more or less worry to the officials having charge of him. (From The *Republican*, Feb. 11, 1926)

Anderson Sent to the House of Correction

"Ralph Anderson, found guilty in the United States District Court at Baltimore recently of attempting to rob the post office at Swanton, this county, two or three months ago, was sentenced to the Chicago House of Correction, a Federal institution, until he becomes twenty-one years old by U.S. Judge Soper in the Federal District Court at Baltimore on last Thursday afternoon. Anderson gave his age as nineteen.

"A similar charge against Henderson Hall, the negro principal in the holdup, was settled, District Attorney A.W.W. Woodcock, announced at the time Judge Soper passed sentence upon Anderson. Shot in the head during the attempted robbery, Hall has become unbalanced and probably will be placed in a State institution. Hall is still held in the Cumberland jail.

"Anderson was arrested September 18 by Deputy Sheriff William D. Casteel, charged with being the accomplice of Hall in the attempted robbery of the post office at Swanton on the night of September 16. Anderson contended that he took no active part in the affair, but that he acted as lookout for Hall while the latter broke into the building.

"The negro, Hall, as The *Republican* reader will remember,

was surprised by Postmaster Joseph F. Friend and a pistol battle followed during which Hall was shot through the stomach and in the face, the bullet fired into his face penetrating his brain. Friend was also struck by a bullet, the missile lodging in his face and destroying one eye. He also sustained a number of lacerations about his head and face when the negro used his revolver as a mace.

"Hall was brought to Oakland the morning following the attempted robbery, his arrest being made by Sheriff Guy O. Yutzy and Deputy Casteel, the prisoner being brought to the Oakland jail by the officers. His condition being of such nature on account of the wounds he had received he was later taken to the Western Maryland Hospital in Cumberland where he was kept under guard for about a month recovering sufficiently by October 22 to be taken to the Allegany County jail where he has remained since his physical recovery. His mental condition however, is such that he will probably be sent to a State institution in a short time." (From The *Republican*, Feb. 25, 1926)

The Governor Thomas House

by Ross C. Durst

A great deal has been written regarding the fact that Governor Thomas built a magnificent house at Frankville and lived there for a short time while attempting to acclimate a drove of Alpaca sheep from Peru. His tragic death there upon the railroad tracts has so firmly linked his name with Frankville that it is not generally known that he lived a much longer period at New Germany. This phase of his colorful career has been generally overlooked by the historians.

Governor Francis Thomas was a brilliant scholar, orator and statesman. He spent nearly a quarter of a century in the congress of the United States. He married the equally cultured and talented daughter of Governor Mc-Dowell of Virginia. This marriage added power and prestige to his rapidly rising star. He was elected as Governor of the state of Maryland after a tumultuous campaign during which he fought a duel with William Price. This dual seems only to have added to his stature. It was freely predicted that he was destined to become the next President of the United States.

Governor Thomas

Then suddenly his world toppled and fell, brought down by his own hand. He chose the morning of his inauguration as governor to announce that he was asking for a divorce from Mrs. Thomas. He had a bill introduced in the State legislature for that purpose. In this modern day, that may seem like getting divorce the hard way but it was the accepted method at that time. Divorces were not as easily secured in those days as they are at present. He had printed and broadcast across the state, a pamphlet in which he set forth his suspicions and charges against his wife.

It has been said that such was his mastery of rhetoric, that after a first reading one was left with the impression that here was a deeply wronged husband and a faithless wife.

However, a second and more critical reading failed to divulge a single grain of fact or evidence of his charges. It would seem that the members of the legislature must have taken a second look. At any rate, the bill failed passage. Whereupon, Mrs. Tho-

Spot where governor was killed.

mas had a similar bill introduced into the legislature of Virginia. This was promptly passed and the divorce granted to Mrs. Thomas. She later remarried and there was left no hope of reconciliation. In later life, Governor Thomas bitterly reproached himself for his actions and attempted to round up all of the pamphlets and destroy them.

His term as Governor (1841-1844) must have been a bitter one. At its conclusion, he chose the life of a recluse. The site of his seclusion was at New Germany, then a very remote section with only a few settlers. Dense forests were almost unbroken except for an occasional settler's cabin.

For years he had been buying large tracts and Military Lots of virgin timberland in what was later to become Garrett County. At the time of his retirement he owned a strip of land about thirty miles long lying along Meadow Mountain and the slopes draining into the Savage River. His holdings amounted to about fifty thousand acres. In the midst of this vast domain at New Germany he built a house in a grove of white pine. While not as commodious as the house built later in life at Mont Alta, it was still a large and comfortable house for a bitter hermit. The prop-

37

erty was later known as Joel Wiland Farm.

For many years, he had no contact with the world he had known except an occasional meeting with the hardy settlers who had drifted across the line from Pennsylvania. My grandfather was one of those settlers living on the eastern slope of Meadow Mountain.

The boundaries of most of the land purchased by Governor Thomas existed only on paper. As a consequence, he soon found himself involved in disputed boundary claims, squatters and expensive law suits. Since he had no income at that time, he eventually found his position too unbearable. He sold the entire holdings to a cousin, Gen. Joseph R. Anderson from Richmond, Virginia, retaining only a tract of 410 acres near Frankville.

While Governor Thomas' long voluntary exile at New Germany is said to have produced a few peculiar aberrations of the mind, it is also true that it served to clarify his mind on many other matters. When the ominous rumbles of a Civil War were heard he came out of retirement. All his ties were with the South, but he saw clearly the danger of such a strife. Living in Maryland, he dwelt in an area that had very divided sympathies between the North and the South, yet he was able to raise a regiment of 3,000 soldiers to fight for the North. Called the "Potomac Home Brigade," the regiment had a large contingent of men from the western part of the state. William Uphole was a member of the infantry unit, and it was through the PHB that he came into contact with Francis Thomas. Uphole returned to the Swanton area after the war. Thomas and Anderson became partners in a saw mill, and eventually bought land near Frankville. Uphole moved to Frankville to work for Thomas.

His zeal for the cause of the Federacy again brought him before the eyes of the public, and after an absence of 20 years, he was again elected to Congress in 1861, and was continuously reelected for several terms--his last term ending March 3, 1869. During the War period he had thus become the dictator of the Republican party in Western Maryland. As a reward for service to the administration, President Grant, in 1870, appointed him Collector of Internal Revenue for the District of Maryland, and two years later sent him as Minister to Peru, which office he held until 1875, when he resigned.

In Peru, Thomas had become interested in Alpaca sheep, and

brought a number to Maryland, hoping to propagate them. Upon his return to Maryland he retired to his farm locally known as "Thomas' Hermitage" in the vastness of the Allegany mountains. Here he had formally purchased a tract of land containing about 2,000 acres, intending to go into an extensive lumber business. He had built quite an extensive system of tram way for getting the logs down to the tracks of the Baltimore and Ohio Railway. But, like every other business enterprise he had undertaken, the lumber business yielded him little profit.

While in Peru, he had caught the idea that his mountain farm would be well adapted to sheep raising, and he entered into this venture with the same enthusiasm that had marked his political career. For more than a year Maryland's once famous political leader buried himself in this wild region, emerging only occasionally to attend to necessary business matters.

Killed by Train

Then suddenly, on January 23, 1876, the country was shocked by notice of his death. While crossing the railroad track, about a mile east of Frankville Station, he was struck by an eastbound "helper" engine coming down the seventeen mile grade. At the time of the accident, he was almost seventy-seven years old.

On the day of his death, he had a group of men cutting locust fence posts on the land along Crabtree Creek below the B&O Railroad embankment. It was Saturday afternoon, and he was walking down the westbound railroad track from Frankville with the intention of giving the men their pay. William Uphole, an employee said that Thomas was walking with his hands behind him, head down, in a thoughtful stance. As the westbound train approached, he stepped over into the center of the eastbound tracks, unaware of the approaching of the "helper" engine. Crew members on the "helper" engine were unable to stop the locomotive before it hit the ex-governor.

A handcar was procured, and Thomas' body was taken to Frankville Station, and then carried to his farmhouse. As soon as intelligence of his death reached the outside world, the Baltimore and Ohio Railroad Company tendered a special train to be taken to Frankville to convey his body to Cumberland. In the gentlemen's reading room in the north wing of the Queen City Hotel, Thomas lay in state. Hundreds of those who had known him and honored him passed by his bier, now recalling his many admirable qualities, and thinking charitably of the eccentricities which had cast their shadow across an otherwise successful life.

On Monday, a funeral service was conducted at Emmanuel Episcopal Church, and on Tuesday a special train took the ex-governor's body to Frederick County for burial.

It has been said that Governor Thomas wrote his own epitaph. On an imposing monument in the churchyard of St. Mark's Episcopal Church, near Petersville, Frederick County, Maryland is found this inscription:

"Ex-Governor Francis Thomas, born Feb. 3, 1799. Died Jan. 23, 1876. Son of Colonel John Thomas and his wife, Eleanor McGill. The author of the measure which gave to Maryland the Constitution of 1864 and thereby gave freedom to 90,000 human beings."

Historical Interest

There has always been historical interest in Ex-Governor Francis Thomas. He was well liked and respected. Often referred to as "Maryland's Grand Old Man," he was looking forward to more years in Garrett County at the time he was killed.

The late Robert Garrett, along with some members of the Historical Society, traveled to Frankville in 1970, to see if anything remained of the "Thomas Hermitage." In a letter written to Mr. Charles A. Jones, he gives the following information.

"Some of us went to the old Governor Thomas place the other day. Two men of that area met us and showed us the site of his house far up on Savage Mountain. These two men knew the house as youngsters, and I was surprised when they said it was torn down as recently as about 1930, when the Savage River Dam was first under construction."

"There still remains part of a log stable, but no other buildings whatever. We assumed that this was where the Governor housed the Peruvian sheep that he brought over from Peru, not long before he was killed."

"The little station, Frankville, on the 17 mile grade,. . .was torn down many years ago. One of our guides retained the station sign, and will lend it to our museum for display."

"The Governor had much of the surrounding hillside cleared and under cultivation, but now it is covered with timber. A number of fruit trees still remain, some of them dating back to his time."

Dr. Conn, Oakland's First Physician, Mysteriously Shot

(Note: Books dealing with the early history of Oakland report "The first doctor to establish his office in Oakland was Dr. John H. Conn, in 1851. His office was located on the corner of Second and Oak streets. In 1854, he was mysteriously shot, as he stood on the steps of his office. Since the affair has been closed for more than a century, perhaps a fuller account is in order.)

"When in 1851, Dr. John H. Conn began the practice of medicine in the young, lusty town of Oakland, he was greeted enthusiastically by the few hundred persons who had built their homes and businesses near the recently completed Baltimore and Ohio railroad tracks.

"The presence of a real practitioner was one more indication that the little settlement had a 'future' this must surely be so if a professional person had cast his lot with the handful of shop keepers and mechanics who had grand plans for the future of their community.

"And grand plans they were. Not only was the railroad bringing people and commerce to the area but there was talk of un-

41

limited coal and timber resources to be developed. Some even visioned the day when the western tip of Maryland would become a self-governing county, like that of Allegany, of which it was a part.

"Of course, it was true that Dr. Conn was a quiet man not given to speaking of himself or his activities before selecting Oakland as his place of practice. But he was young; he was personable and he had capable-qualities enough, the citizens decided, in any newcomer. Besides, he was the only physician in the entire area, the nearest being Dr. John H. Patterson, in Grantsville-a long, hard ride to the north in time of need.

"Dr. Conn set up his office in a small building on the corner of what is now Second and Oak streets, and from the beginning his practice flourished. In the days before the convenience of a well-stocked pharmacy, it was said that the 'young doctor' either had on hand the correct medication, or could prescribe a suitable home remedy for any attack of ague or vapors, vague ailments which were popular in that period.

"The presence in the community of a handsome young doctor, with a somewhat mysterious past naturally was not overlooked by the young ladies-the married as well as the single.

"One of the former was Ann Johnson, whose husband, Cornelius, operated a thriving general store on Railroad Street, just a stone's throw from the office of the new doctor.

"Mrs. Johnson some years younger than her husband, was pictured as a particularly unhappy woman. Reared in the social climes of the cities to the east, she detested life in what she described as 'this outpost of civilization.' Further, she felt her hard-working husband was more interested in his barrels of flour and bolts of materials than in his socially-conscious wife.

"While social activities in the young community were extremely limited, 'that Johnson woman,' as the town gossips described her, took advantage of every opportunity to make the young physician conscious of her presence. And while the doctor was polite enough he privately confided that he found her attentions distasteful.

"From the apartment over her husband's store, Mrs. Johnson could observe the comings and goings of the doctor and his patients, for the office was a scant 300 feet distant. It was to be expected, perhaps, that the young lady found many excuses over the months following to visit the office professionally, either for herself or with her infant daughter.

"For Mr. and Mrs. Johnson were the parents of one child, a daughter whom this vain, elegant, extra ordinary mother had blessed with the improbable name of Ida Lucy Florence Jeanette Genevieve Jenny Lind Johnson.

"As time passed, and the visits continued, Mrs. Johnson was convinced that her personality and charm were making an impression on Dr. Conn. True, he showed no sign of interest except that required by his professional services but who she reasoned, could resist the charm of the city-bred social leader of this impossible backwoods community.

"At a time when she believed her charm and beauty were capturing everyone, particularly the doctor, the cruel blow fell. A friend reported that Dr. Conn, far from impressed, had actually described her as a 'butterfly fool.' Just imagine her chagrin.

"Here, then, was the perfect setting for an ante-bellum soap opera. We have:

"The stodgy, hard-wording husband, chained to his business, concerned more with the safe arrival of a wagon-load of merchandise from the east than the social aspiration of his young wife;

"The handsome young doctor, more concerned with the welfare of his patients and the building of his practice than the advances of a 'butterfly fool';

"And, finally, the lonely, frustrated wife, who had rudely discovered herself to be, in the doctor's opinion, of no personal interest at all!

"In short, a woman scorned! And in Oakland, as elsewhere, there can be no such fury!

"Sitting in her apartment, day after day, watching the doctor's office, Mrs. Johnson planted the seeds of revenge. It is probably an insight into her mental condition to realize that she decided only the doctor's life could atone for the imagined 'insult' she had suffered.

"Lacking the courage of the deed, she turned to her husband to act as executioner. Who can surmise, over a century later, what tales the young matron told the man to turn him from the patient shop keeper into the blood-seeking 'husband wronged'?

"At any rate, a plan evolved. Mrs. Johnson noted that every evening at seven o'clock Dr. Conn entered his office, passing briefly to unlock the door. From the vantage point of her living room window, the doctor's wide back presented a perfect target, within easy range of even a mediocre rifleman.

"She, together with her husband, selected the date for the murder as an evening in the early spring of 1854. On that evening, Cornelius Johnson left the store in the hands of his wife a few minutes before seven, climbed the stairs to his apartment and primed his muzzle-loader. Glancing out of the window toward the doctor's office, he saw a figure awaiting the physician's arrival.

"'Complications,' he thought, as he recognized Marquis Perry, one of Conn's patients.

"Marquis, who was a slight man extremely timid, had been undergoing treatment of nervous disorders and was a regular patient. At about this moment, Johnson saw the figure of Dr. Conn approach, speak briefly with Perry, and turn to unlock the door.

"One shot was fired and the doctor crumbled at the step. The bullet passed through his head and lodged in the office door.

"There was no opportunity for a second try. Poor, nervous Marquis, hearing the blast and seeing the physician fall, took off in a dead trot for home, where he hid himself in a closet.

"It remained for others to move Dr. Conn to Thayer's saloon, on Railroad Street, where he was pronounced dead by Constable Thomas Arnold, the only representative of the law in the vicinity.

"Following a brief investigation, Arnold entered the Johnson store, where he found Cornelius and his wife going about their business. He placed the man under arrest for murder, and Johnson was subsequently tried in Cumberland for the crime.

"Here, the case attracted wide attention, but in those days before scientific methods of crime detection, the deed was difficult to prove. The only witnesses the prosecution could summon were Mrs. Johnson, who steadfastedly refused to testify against her husband, and Marquis Perry, who had been too frightened to retain a coherent memory of the affair. The entire incident, he is reported as testifying 'did not tend to improve my nervous condition.'

"A jury failed to find Johnson guilty, due to lack of witnesses and evidence, and here the later activities of Mr. and Mrs.

Johnson become difficult to trace.

"Following his trial, Johnson apparently gave up his mercantile business in Oakland and disappeared from the local scene. The business site was later used as the Davis Millinery shop until it was destroyed in the fire of July 14, 1898, as related several weeks ago.

"Mrs. Johnson, however, continued to live in the apartment with her young daughter for some time longer. One day she left the infant in the care of a neighbor, Mrs. White, stating that she was going out to perform some errands. Instead, she walked to the depot, boarded the east bound passenger train, and so far as can be determined was heard from no more.

"And no more information can be secured concerning the fate of the young daughter, Ida Lucy Florence Jeanette Genevieve Jenny Lind Johnson." (The *Republican* February 2, 1961)

Removal of Windlass Recalls Tragedy

"The old windlass that has stood over the well by the side entrance of the court house for many years, is gone, never to be replaced. Oscar Notes, janitor at the court house, was busy one day last week taking down the familiar old sight, and putting in its place, a covering with green paint which didn't make the place look anything like it did before, but supposedly a little safer.

"The demolition of the windlass has brought to mind a tragedy that happened there many years ago, so many years ago that very few residents of Oakland are aware that anything like a tragedy hinged upon that one little well. But there is a story connected with it, and several residents in those days remember quite distinctly what took place.

"About 1877, the site where the court house now stands was occupied by a two story structure, called the Beer Garden, and

45

owned and operated by a Mr. Corrigan. Corrigan's Beer Garden is said to have been quite a popular place in those days.

"An old negro man, Ely Truly was his name, who was at that time past middle age of life, was the janitor of the Beer Garden, and it was his wont to make many trips to the well each day. On one occasion he went out during the evening to get a bucket of water. Whether or not he was filled with the substance after which the establishment was named is a question, but he lost his balance and fell into the well. He was discovered shortly after and a great excitement was caused over the accident. It is not known whether he was killed by contact against the sides of the well, or whether he drowned.

"There is a marker in the Oakland cemetery over the grave of Ely Truly, who was buried there.

"The well was still used for drinking purposes until about fourteen years ago when it was closed on account of typhoid fever germs. Mr. William Maffett, who was sheriff in 1913, took typoid fever from drinking some of this water and shortly afterwards it was considered closed. Mr. Maffett died from the effect fourteen years ago yesterday.

"At the time of the negro's death, there were about 800 inhabitants in the town of Oakland, according to E.Z. Tower, clerk of the circuit court. He remembers distinctly the occasion of the accident and says that enough excitement was caused by that to satiate the town for a number of days.

"He thinks that the negro was out by the well cleaning 'spittoons' when he lost his balance and fell in. If that is the case, the well had a right to finally become polluted.

"But the well has been closed permanently now, and everyone who enters the side door of the court house, notices something lacking. The scenery doesn't look the same, and probably never will to the older residents who are accustomed to entering the building from Alder Street." (Article from June 1927 issue of The *Republican*)

The next week's issue of The *Republican* carried this follow-up story.

Pittsburgh Subscriber Sees Story of Tragedy of Ely Truly in *Republican*; Writes Account

"Mrs. Ida J. Crim, residing in Pittsburgh, has written a letter to the Editor of The *Republican* in connection with the feature article appearing in last week's issue of the paper in regard to the drowning of Ely Truly, a negro, in the well by the side entrance of the Court House. She was a personal witness of the accident and feels very much interested in getting the facts straight to the public.

"'As I was right on the spot when poor old uncle Ely met his fate,' she writes, 'I couldn't resist writing this enclosed article as there seems to be some doubt in the minds of some of the old timers about the eventful happening as to the dates, etc. But every little detail of the sad occurrence has remained in my mind and always will.'"

Following is the enclosed article:

"'I was deeply interested in the article printed in last week's issue of The *Republican* referring to the drowning accident which befell Ely Truly, an old colored man, well known in Oakland for many years. The property adjoining the Corrigan Beer Garden mentioned in the article and being the principal portion of the ground on which the Court House now stands, was owned and occupied as a family residence by my father, the late Joseph M. Crim, and family for forty years. During this time, all the water consumed by our family was drawn from this old well where Ely Truly met his fate, as well as by neighbors far and near. Old Uncle Ely, as we children called him, passed our home many times a day with two large sized tin buckets carrying water from the old Corrigan well for Miss Della Edwards, corner of Fourth and Oak Streets, who gave him a home. It was on Christmas eve, 1877, at five o'clock. I just came out of my home to go to the well, when Uncle Ely passed by our gate (with the familiar buckets) in a badly intoxicated condition. He got to the well in advance of me and was drawing the well bucket up (one of those heavy iron-bound ones containing water sufficient to fill two buckets of domestic size.) While trying to pull the bucket to the platform, he released his grip on the windlass handle, and Uncle Ely, bucket, windlass rope and all went down. All I could see when I looked down was the bottom of his shoes as they disappeared under the water. His body was recovered that night at 9:30 by the use of grappling hooks. Great excitement reigned in Oakland that night. (Signed) Ida C. Crim'"

Found in *Republican* Files

After the date of the accident was so certain in the mind of Mrs. Crim, the issue of The *Republican* following the mishap was looked over and an account of the accident was found. Volume 1, number 44, dated Saturday, December 29, 1877, had the following to say:

"Drowned in Well

"Saturday evening last about half past five o'clock, Ely Truly, colored, while drawing water from Mr. Corrigan's well, in Oakland, lost his balance and plunged, head first, into the well, and before assistance could be rendered, was drowned. The well is about sixty feet deep, and contained about twenty-five feet of water at the time of the accident. The body was drawn out, after a lapse of half an hour, and conveyed to the residence of

Miss Edwards, where the deceased had been making his home for the past four or five years, and was interred in the Odd Fellows' cemetery on Monday. Deceased was a slave in the Bruce family until the late war, through which he served as an officer's servant. He was a quiet, inoffensive man, with more than ordinary intelligence, and had it not been for the use of whiskey, which was the indirect cause of his death, would have been a useful citizen."

Old Stone House
is Rich in History

"On Route 40, three miles east of Grantsville, stands an old stone tavern, as old as the National Pike itself. Cars zoom by it, beckoned on by the romance of the open road ahead, and few notice the big stone house by the way, which is steeped in the romance of the road of the past, before the railroad, when stage coaches and Conestoga wagons lumbered by along that great East-West route over the mountains.

"The Inn was built in 1818 by Jesse Tomlinson, called 'the old Baron,' at Little Meadows, 'a comfortable day's journey from Cumberland.' Even at that time Little Meadows already had historic significance because it was so named by George Washington and had been the site of one of the camps of General Braddock and Major Washington on their march west to meet the French at Fort Duquesne in 1754, during the French and Indian war. The English and Colonial troops again camped at Little Meadows on the retreat from Duquesne, after the death of Braddock.

"When you stand today on the back porch of the inn you look across a great stretch of valley to Meadow Mountain beyond, and to your left in a far field you see the stone-enclosed burial

Stone house of Little Crossing.

ground of the Tomlinson family which contains also the unmarked graves of several soldiers lost in the campaign of the
French and Indian war. Near it is said to be the site of a small
fort erected by George Washington.

"The first thing that impresses you is the great size of the
stones in the walls. They must have been raised in place by
some sort of block and tackle because many of them are over
two and three feet square. Because of these thick walls the window sills inside are over two feet deep. Enormous chimneys are
at each end of the house, thirty feet wide at the base. A wide
green porch has been added along the whitewashed front of the
house, but the two porches in back, upstairs and down, have
always been there. By the lower porch and entrance into the
tavern room stands the watering trough where horses, drivers
and pedestrians could stop for a cooling drink of the constantly
flowing clear spring water and for gossip with the loungers who
sat about the porch in the shade of the grape vine.

"The waters in this valley are said to be very health-giving,
and at one time later in the century, the Stone Tavern enjoyed
gay social seasons when people came from the East to 'take the

50

waters.'

The peak of prosperity for the tavern came about the middle of the century, before the railroad was put through to Wheeling. Then it was the center of a bustling life for many groups, local as well as transient. The inn keeper was a very influential man, consulted and deferred to in the county. Quite often the wagoners, if they were lucky enough, married the tavern keeper's daughter and retired to the business of running an inn. There was a close fraternity of the road, and the Pike boys, or those who lived along the highway, considered themselves very superior to the backwoodsmen.

"Stone Tavern in those days was a small town in itself. There was a post office (the first in Garrett County, established in 1822) and a store in the inn building. Each evening the wagon yard was full of four and six horse teams, their horses left in the traces. One enclosure might contain ten mules and another 1,000 hogs or cattle being driven to market. In the bar room the wagoners, the glamour boys of the Pike, sang songs, told stories, and cursed the railroad. Corn whiskey was three to five cents a glass. When bed time came, the wagoners put their bedding on the floor and slept in a semi-circle, their feet to the fire, the grate which was large enough to burn six bushels of coal.

"In the dining room on the first floor stood a long table, which is still in the inn, where the stage coach passengers ate. The board would be set with mutton, venison, wild turkey, pheasant, and brook trout. These dinners were fifty cents for the stage coach passengers, but drivers and wagoners and others got theirs much cheaper.

"Many famous guests sat down to these dinners. Four presidents were entertained there: President Jackson, President Taylor, President Polk and President-elect Harrison. Henry Clay frequently stopped here, and Jennie Lind, the Swedish nightingale, is said to have stayed at the inn when she was making her triumphal tour. She was accompanied by her manager, P.T. Barnum.

"Naturally, many legends have grown up around a house which has seen as much life as Old Stone House. Some of these are said to be true, others nobody really knows about; all of them are fascinating.

"A man is said to have been killed in one of the bedrooms. The spots of blood still mark the floor; they cannot be erased. Up until a few years ago people still bothered the owners with requests to dig on the property for gold coin which is supposed to have been buried there at the time of the revolution.

"The most intriguing story is about a beautiful, heavily-veiled woman with quantities of expensive luggage bearing foreign labels, who got off the stage to spend the night at Stone House. She had her supper brought to her room and did not once set foot outside of her door. The next morning one of the little servant boys brought her hot water. But she had disappeared. All of her baggage remained, but there was no trace of her. The woods were searched as thoroughly as possible, but she was never found; and to this day no one knows who she was.

"The Old Stone House can still tell many a good tale, but we are too hurried to listen. It sits four-square in solid strength by the highway and will still be there when we have gone on, clear out of the picture. There is something very sad about its position, still so close to the road it served, but so remote from the present life of that road." (The *Republican* August 16, 1951)

Woman Outwits Sheriff and Outruns Deputies

"After assuring Sheriff William D. Casteel that she would appear before the nearest magistrate Monday and there furnish bond for her appearance in court in answer to the charge of having moonshine whiskey in her home, Mrs. John Doe,* resident of the Bear Hill section of Garrett County, refuted her contract, for as the sheriff and his deputies were leaving the neighborhood she appeared on the brow of a distant hill and told them in strident tones that she had changed her mind and that if they wanted her to 'come and get me.'

"Bear Hill is located north of Bittinger and has long been the stronghold of 'shiners'--men and women. The woman's intimacy with the lay of the country copied with the fact that she is fleet of foot, gave her an advantage, according to Sheriff Casteel, and it was impossible to overtake her. The woman was without shoes, but that fact did not appear to handicap her in traveling over the stony ground and through the brush."

First Violation Under New Law

"This was the first known violation of the new public local law prohibiting the manufacture of liquor which went into effect on June 1st. The law is applicable to Garrett County only and its penalties are severe.

"Section 1 of the law provides 'that it shall be unlawful for any person, association or corporation to manufacture any spirituous or fermented liquors within the limits of Garrett County, Maryland,' and provides a penalty of a fine and confinement in the House of Correction.

"Following information received, the Sheriff and his deputies called at the home of the Doe family early on last Sunday morning. The sheriff had a warrant for Doe, who is charged with being only one of the many moonshiners of the Bear Hill section.

"The Doe family had not yet risen when the officers approached the house but their loud knocking at the door aroused Mrs. Doe, who for a time refused them entrance. Upon gaining admission, after considerable parley with the woman, a search was made for Doe. They were unable to find him. However, in going through the dwelling they discovered eight gallons of alleged moonshine, which was contained in fruit jars.

"Following the uncovering of the contraband, Mrs. Doe was placed under arrest, but protested against being taken into custody, saying that she had no shoes and could not walk the mile or more from her place to the point where the Sheriff had left his car. She is also said to have had the care of a very young child.

"Upon her promise to appear at the office of the nearest magistrate on Monday morning and furnish bond, the officer permitted her to remain at her home. Sometime later, stated the Sheriff, Mrs. Doe appeared barefoot on the top of a hill and called to him declaring that she had changed her mind and would not appear on Monday as promised.

"She was ordered to be taken into custody but the woman fled and the men following were unable to overtake her. Due to the roughness of the ground and the apparent agility of the barefoot woman, the officers were therefore compelled to return to Oakland with only a jar of 'shine' as evidence." (From June 16, 1927 issue of The *Republican*. *Name changed throughout article.)

Nancy Hufford Wiley

Brown's Miscellaneous Writings by Jacob Brown, and *Pioneer Families* by Capt. Charles Hoye, both mention Nancy Hufford, and Holmes Wiley. Holmes Oliver Wiley was one of Garrett County's noted hunters, he was born in 1800 and died at the age of seventy-eight years. A remarkable man in many respects, and a farmer by vocation, he much preferred the rifle and the hunt, and enjoyed the sport throughout a long life.

Holmes Wiley and his first wife, Elizabeth Yeast, daughter of John Yeast, raised ten children. After her death, Holmes married Nancy Hufford. Nancy was tried and acquitted in 1851 of the charge of poisoning Mrs. Engle. Nancy was the daughter of William and Sally Woodin, both of whom are buried in the Grantsville cemetery. Woodin originally from Howard County, Maryland, operated an inn at Little Crossings, later moving to Tomlinson's Stone House Inn, and finally to Smooth Valley where he was operating an inn and general store at the time of death. He died on December 13, 1834, at the age of fifty-six years. Sally died March 7, 1843, at sixty years of age. When William Woodins' estate was settled, it listed his daughter as Nancy Layman.

Nancy's first husband was John Yeast, a man of splendid

physique, enjoying perfect health and strength, yet death came in early manhood. He was thirty-six years old when he died on July 22, 1833, with grave suspicions of foul play. Insidious poison supposed to be the cause of his sudden death, the wife in later years strongly suspected of being the author of his death as well as other similar ones. John was buried in the Grantsville cemetery.

Seven months after the death of John Yeast, a marriage license was issued for Nancy Yeast and John Layman on March 6, 1834. John, the member of a prosperous and highly-respected family, also operated an inn on the National Road. The ten years following Nancy's marriage to John were quite uneventful, then on September 23, 1845, John Layman died, still a comparatively young man. His will probated October 14, 1845, named his wife, Nancy, as heir to all his real estate, which included land and the tavern called "The Woodin Estate."

On February 9, 1848, Allegany County Clerk of Court issued a marriage license to Samuel Hufford and Nancy Layman. By the time the final accounting of John Layman's will on October 8, 1850, was made, Nancy Woodin Yeast Layman Hufford was a woman of considerable wealth. Samuel Hufford did not live very long after his marriage with Nancy, for on October 22, 1851, a bench warrant was issued for her arrest, she was identified as "spinster" and later in the Grand Jury report as "widow". The warrant was marked as "State of Maryland vs. Nancy Hufford for the murder of Mrs. Rebecca Engle, by feloniously administering poison, commonly called White Arsenic."

Rebecca Engle was the ninth child of Charles and Mary M. (Beaver) Broadwater. Rebecca was the second wife of Samuel Engle, his first wife Elizabeth having died on September 28, 1848, age thirty-five years, seven months and ten days. Rebecca died October 2, 1851 age twenty-nine years, four months and twenty-four days. In the autumn of 1851, Samuel and Rebecca had their first child, Martha Engle. Nancy Hufford came to the Engle household on September 22, to help Mrs. Engle. She remained until October 2, when Mrs. Engle died. Mrs. Engle became violently ill on September 22. Two doctors had her under their care, and Nancy took great care in fixing tea, and milk toast which she would coax Rebecca to swallow. Poisoning did not occur to the doctors attending Rebecca, until old memories were stirred by other such deaths in the neighborhood, always in the wake of Nancy. It might have been supposed that she had designs on Samuel Engle, and eventually his property, as he was a very wealthy man. If so, she misjudged her prey, as Samuel Engle accused her of the murder of Rebecca.

A post-mortem was conducted on the body of Rebecca Engle the day after her death. Some days later the body was again reexamined. The first examination was of the stomach and contents, the second was of the liver, and other organs, poison being very hard to detect. White arsenic was a powder, resembling flour or powdered sugar. When mixed with food it is almost tasteless. It dissolves freely in boiling water or when mixed with alkaline substances. It would have been a rare farm home which did not have a supply of white arsenic, commonly used as rat poison.

The Grand Jury charged her with murder, the second count was the same except the means of administering the poison to Mrs. Engle. In the third count it was Nancy's alleged method of mixing the poison in tea that Rebecca drank. To all counts in the indictment Nancy pleaded "Not guilty". The state called eighteen witnesses against Nancy, her lawyers called twelve people testifying for Nancy, eleven men and one woman, the woman being Nancy's sister, Sarah Yeast, the widow of Peter Yeast who had died suddenly at the age of forty-two, in June 1851, just five months prior to the trial. The jury did not convict her, and the verdict was "Not Guilty."

After the trial Nancy was in reduced circumstances, much of her property went to pay her lawyers. In the meantime, Samuel Engle took as his third wife Catherine Hoye Ridgely in March of 1854. Catherine who was the daughter of William W. Hoye and his wife, Eleanor Slicer, had been married before to William Ridgely in November of 1846. It was a very short marriage as William's will was probated on December 29, 1848. For a number of years it seemed as though Nancy had completely dropped out of sight, but on April 23, 1862 a marriage license was issued for Holmes Wiley, the hunter, widower and property owner. The fact of the matter was that through his first wife, Elizabeth Yeast, daughter of John Yeast, Nancy had been Holmes Wiley's step-mother-in-law.

The years between 1862 and 1871 were quiet years for Holmes

and Nancy, with nothing more eventful than the sale of property for both he and Nancy, to various people. Holmes Wiley died on his farm in 1878, and was buried beside his first wife on the Wiley farm near Bittinger. His son Thomas B. Wiley administered the final account for Holmes estate on January 2, 1882. Since there was no mention of Nancy we must assume that she had predeceased her husband.

No tombstone for Nancy Woodin Yeast Layman Hufford Wiley, was ever found. However, further research disclosed that she was buried beside Holmes Wiley and his first wife, on the Wiley farm, all are buried in unmarked graves. According to the local rumors, it was thought that Holmes Wiley's first wife died of poisoning.

Nancy apparently began her married life in Allegany County, Maryland, and ended it in Garrett County, Maryland, as Garrett County was established in 1872. Did Nancy really poison the people as suspected, or was it all coincidence?

Daniel Mosser Shot by Mabel Swann

Daniel Mosser

The shooting of Daniel Mosser was a closely followed event through articles in the local papers in 1927. The saga began with a May 26, 1927, article in The *Republican* newspaper and ended with a February 2, 1928, article in the same

Deputy Joy Griffith with murder gun.

paper.

"Mabel Swann, said to be a graduate nurse, is under arrest charged with having shot and killed Daniel Mosser, of Keyser, WVa., about ten o'clock this morning. The shooting took place at the Mosser farm, near Swanton, upon which the Swann woman has been a tenant for several months.

"On Monday following information received by the local and Federal prohibition officers, the place was raided where several hundred gallons of

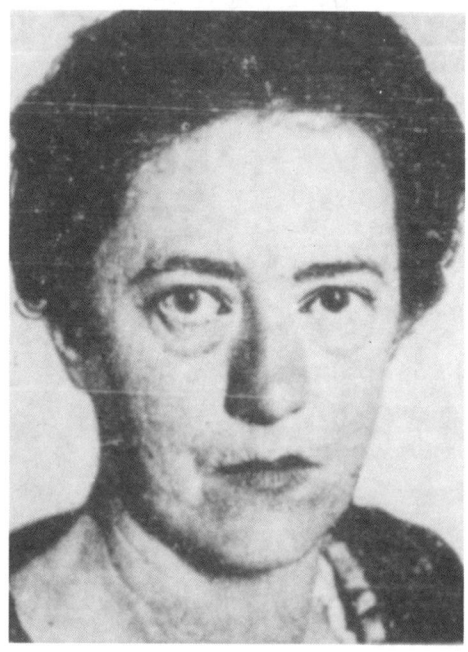
Mabel Swann

mash, about five gallons of liquor and a coil were found under a tent, and destroyed. It is presumed by the officers that Mosser, hearing of the raid went to the farm to rid it of the undesirable tenant and a quarrel ensued, followed by the shooting.

"Mosser was employed as a hostler in the Keyser shops of the Baltimore and Ohio Railroad. He worked last night and arrived at Swanton about nine o'clock this morning going to the farm at once.

"At ten o'clock the Swann woman appeared at the Swanton railroad station and requested the agent to telephone Sheriff

Sheriff William D. Casteel

Casteel to 'come to her place at once and to bring a doctor with him, as she had shot Dan Mosser, but did not know whether he was dead or not.'

"The sheriff left immediately. A few minutes afterward a second message was received announcing Mosser's death. The dead man was aged 40 years, and he is survived by his wife and four children.

"The Swann woman is considered an eccentric character. She always dressed like a man, wearing knee-high gum boots and made a living by driving a coal or lumber wagon as occasion required. It is said that upon one occasion she was heard to remark that two things would not be tolerated on her farm--a man and a hog.

"Sheriff Casteel upon going to the Mosser place, found the woman, who gave herself up, and who stated that the dead man had tried to break into the house to collect the rent due him; that she had shot him with a .22 caliber rifle and apparently does not regret the deed.

The officer brought his prisoner to Oakland, and she is now in jail. An inquest will be held this afternoon to be conducted by Justice Gonder, who will impanel the jury."

Swann Awaiting Trial Tells Her Story

"Mabel Swann, charged with having shot and killed Daniel Mosser, last Thursday morning at her farm is in jail, and is calmly awaiting her trial, which will come up at the June term of court to convene next Monday. She will be charged with murder. During her stay in jail, she has persisted in her story that she shot in self-defense.

"Tuesday evening when questioned about the alleged murder, she refused at first to give further information than had already been given out. Later she began: 'It was purely accidental. There was nothing else to do. The man broke into the house through the only door and was rushing toward me very fast. I did not know what he would have done, and there was no escape. I had to shoot to save myself. There was nothing premeditated about it.'

"Mosser, according to her story, had no right in the first place to rent her the farm as it was held jointly by him and his sister, who resides in Cumberland. The sister, she says, wrote her a letter telling her not to pay Mosser any money until May 30, when all the family was to gather together at Swanton for a picnic. The fact that Mosser had heard of this was given by the Swann woman as the reason for his attack upon her home in an attempt to force the rent money from her.

"When asked about the corn mash and moonshine found in her house, she exclaimed: 'If there was any evidence of liquor in the house it was put there. The many people of Oakland with whom I am acquainted know that I never touched moonshine and never had anything to do with it.'

"The Swann woman went on to explain that Mosser had always kept one room in the house for his own in which harness, furniture and a lot of other property was stored. She declared that she had never been in the room but once and that was after the raid in which moonshine and mash was discovered in

60

there. According to Sheriff Casteel, liquor was found not only in that one room but in the kitchen and under the mattress of one of the beds.

"The body of Mosser, whom she asserts was shot in the front room of the house, was found in the yard about ten feet from the steps when Sheriff Casteel arrived. A stream of blood led from the house to where the body lay.

"Mabel Swann came to Oakland four years ago from Baltimore and lived for a short time on a farm near Oakland before moving to the Swanton area."

Swan Case Removed to Cumberland For Trial

"The court Tuesday morning ordered the murder trial of Miss Mabel Swann charged with slaying Daniel Mosser, to be removed from Oakland to Cumberland where she will be tried during the October term of the Circuit court of Allegany County. Attorneys David A. Robb, of Cumberland, and William R. Offutt of Oakland, defense counsel, asked for change, claiming that it was impossible to secure an impartial trial for her in Oakland, due to public sentiment against the woman. Judge D.L. Sloan granted the change. She will remain in jail pending the reopening of the trial.

"A plea of self-defense will be entered, according to her counsel. 'She shot Mosser only after he had threatened her life and thrown a brick at her,' one of the counsel said. While there are no witnesses who actually saw the murder committed, there will be a score or more who will take the stand to testify that threats against Mosser were made by her prior to the shooting.

"The greatest number of people ever to attend court was present Tuesday, expecting to hear the case. She was taken to the court room in the afternoon where she was arraigned.

"Although said to be penniless a week ago, she has apparently become the beneficiary of mysterious friends, because funds for her defense have appeared from some unknown source, and notes on which she had borrowed money for her stock have been paid. The officers state that they have no idea as to the source of the money. It was hinted to newspaper reporters several days ago in an interview with her that she had sources from which financial aid could be obtained, but would not divulge the place or the people."

Trial of Mabel Swann Begins in Cumberland

"The trial of Mabel Swann began early Monday morning on October 24, 1927, at the Allegany County Courthouse, Cumberland. The trial was hotly contested by both sides. Prosecuting the case were Julius C. Renninger, States' Attorney for Garrett County, William A. Huster, State's Attorney for Allegany County, and E.R. Jones, Oakland attorney. Miss Swann was defended by Fuller Barnard, Jr., former Judge W.C. Walsh, David A. Robb and William R. Offutt. There were thirty-two witnesses for the State, including those who were on the scene immediately after the shooting, physicians who examined the body of Mosser, Sheriff Casteel of Garrett County, and his deputy, Joy Griffith. The trial attracted many people, the courtroom being crowded to capacity.

"State's Attorney Julius C. Renninger asked for a verdict of murder in the first degree. After reading various authorities recognized in the Maryland courts dealing with murder and homicide, he reviewed the case. The farm which Miss Swann rented from Mosser was the old Mosser home, he said. Mosser, who lived in Keyser, Mr. Renninger stated, came by train from Keyser to Swanton, about a mile from the farm, on the morning of May 26. About nine o'clock he went up to the farm, seeking rental money. He had with him a receipt, prepared by Mrs. Mosser. He met several men on the way, it was stated. These men appeared as witnesses Monday afternoon.

"C. O'Brien, a farmer of the vicinity, and Virgie Wilt, a mail carrier, were those he passed on the way. Later on in the day, Arlie Johnson, a timber hauler, while coming down the road, happened to glance in the direction of the farm. He saw, the State's Attorney said, a man lying in a strange position in the yard near the porch. When Johnson testified, he corroborated the State's Attorney's statements. Johnson then went on to Swanton. When he returned, he testified, he saw a large crowd gathered in the yard of the farm.

"A number of witnesses testified to seeing the body of Mosser lying on the ground, a bullet wound in the chest. After Miss Swann had shot Mosser she mounted a horse and rode to Swanton, where she informed those whom she happened to meet of the shooting.

"Luther Shank, a brother-in-law of Mosser, was put on the stand during the afternoon session of the court. Although his answers to the questions asked him by the attorneys were rather incoherent and vague, it developed, from his testimony that on April 26, accompanied by Russell Lee, Lester Weimer, Lawton Friend and Joseph Friend, all of whom live in the vicinity of Swanton, he visited Miss Swann at her farm. Meeting her in the yard, he said, he asked if she had any liquor in her possession, which she replied, he said, 'Sure.'

"She told them, Shank declared, that Mosser had been there in the morning, 'raising hell' because she had liquor on the premises. She feared, Shank stated, that Mosser would inform the Federal officers of the presence of the liquor. 'I'm going to shoot the---- next time he acts like that around here,' Shank said Miss Swann told them. She then asked them to help her load the liquor on a wagon to take it away and hide it. This was done, Shank averred, and six gallons were hidden in the woods, while a gallon was given to the young men for their help, the witness testified.

"Lawton Friend, a former merchant of Swanton, who testified in the morning, and Joseph Z. Friend, his younger brother, when placed on the stand, both told substantially the same story as related by Shank.

"Peter Bickford, another witness for the State, declared that he had known Miss Swann for about a year. He said that she had spoken to him about a raid which had been made on her farm the Monday before the shooting. She asked him he said, whether or not he thought that it was the Federal officers who had conducted the raid. Bickford stated that she told him she had heard Mosser was the one who reported her to the authorities and that she said, 'If I find out, I'll kill him.'

"C.C. Mason, a merchant of Swanton, who was near by when

Bickford had his conversation with Miss Swann backed up Bickford's statements. He said that he was helping repair a road on Meadow Mountain at the time.

"Joy Griffith, a deputy sheriff, who was present during the raid Miss Swann referred to in her conversation with Bickford, told the court and jury that he had found a .22 calibre rifle in the house, which was the gun which Miss Swann used in the shooting. The rifle and a number of shells were exhibited in court. The rifle, Griffith said, when he found it during the raid, was very dusty and apparently in a neglected condition. When it was found after the shooting, he said, it had evidently been thoroughly cleaned and oiled up.

"Andrew Shartzer, of Oakland, who testified Monday morning, was placed on the stand again in the afternoon, when he also described the condition of the gun. His description was similar to Griffith's.

"Henry Johnson, a Swanton farmer, testified that he was present at the farm about one o'clock on the day of the shooting. He stated that he saw the body of Mosser and also spots of blood a few feet from the porch of the house. He picked up a .22 calibre shell, he said, three or four feet from the porch, which, he asserted, had the appearance of having lately been fired. The shell was produced in court and he identified it. John McRobie, of Swanton, was also present the day of the shooting, he testified. He stated that he, too, saw the spots of blood, the first spot being about seven feet from the house, according to his testimony. The body was about twenty feet away from the house. McRobie also testified to finding a brick in the house and a broken lamp shade. He was the last witness of the day.

"Dr. N.I. Broadwater, of Oakland, and Dr. H.T. Coffman, of Keyser, were among the first witnesses to be examined after court convened Monday afternoon. Dr. Broadwater saw the body about 12 o'clock on the day of the shooting. It was stretched out on the ground, he said, about 20 feet from the house. The legs were drawn up, he said, and after examining the dead man he found a small bullet wound in upper left part of the chest. Mosser's mouth was full of blood, Dr. Broadwater declared, which was due to the fact that one of the man's lungs had been punctured by the bullet.

"Both physicians said death must have been almost instant.

64

They were questioned to some length by the attorneys. After being examined by David A. Robb, for the defense, it was brought out that the bullet had glanced on the lower part of the third rib. It was shown that the bullet entered the body at an angle, which, the attorneys and physicians said, would indicate that Mosser was either bending over when the bullet hit him or that the person firing the gun was in a higher position than Mosser. Dr. Coffman, who performed the autopsy, stated that when he examined the body it was partly decomposed and covered with a white substance. The wound, he said, which was a clean one, was not difficult to trace.

"The widow of the dead man, Mrs. Daniel Mosser, of Keyser, took the stand late in the afternoon. Mosser, she said left Keyser about 7:30 in the morning of the day of the shooting, taking with him a prepared receipt, which, with the rifle and shell, were offered by the prosecution as evidence.

"Miss Swann, when placed on the stand before testimony was completed, told about the brick which the defense claimed Mosser threw at her. The State contended that Mosser never threw the brick. He never even got to the house on the day of the shooting, the State claimed. Miss Swann explained that she used the brick when mending harnesses. Dr. A.H. Hawkins, who was the first witness summoned yesterday morning, testified that Miss Swann suffered from a toxic goiter, which probably would affect her thyroid gland.

"Deputy Sheriff Joy Griffith was recalled and identified the two pieces of brick which he found in the room the day of the shooting. The large piece, he said, was on the table, and the smaller piece on the floor. The State attempted to show that Miss Swann had used the monkey wrench to break the brick, and then arranged them to look as though Mosser had thrown one of the pieces at her. Joseph Friend and W.A. Gonder also testified to seeing the bricks and brick dust on the monkey wrench. L.D. Shank was put on the stand again and identified the bricks.

"There were frequent objections on the part of the attorneys during the taking of the testimony, and twice the jury was sent out of the court room while the court considered the objections.

"William R. Offutt, in opening for the defense said Monday morning that they would admit the facts concerning the shooting were, in the main, correct. However, he said, the entire affair was an accident and that there was nothing strange in the fact that Miss Swann possessed a rifle.

"Miss Swann, after coming to this section for her health, he said, toiled as a laborer, doing her own farming. Her reputation was flawless, he said. Mr. Offutt said that Mosser who was a large man was extremely disagreeable in his conduct with his tenant and at one time attempted to caress her. He related Miss Swann's actions after the shooting occurred. She rode to Swanton on a horse, he declared, and failing to get aid from several people whom she met there, went to a couple of business places and to the railroad station. When several men did go to the farm, they found Mosser dead.

"Every action and every movement of Miss Swann, Mr. Offutt stated, showed plainly she was innocent of shooting with intent to kill.

"Miss Swann herself was on the witness stand on Tuesday. 'Of course I never made any threats against the life of Dan Mosser. Why should I? He never gave me any serious trouble.' Mabel Swann made this statement Tuesday afternoon when she appeared on the stand as the first witness for the defense. During the testimony there was constant quarreling and wrangling between the attorneys. Miss Swann vigorously denied much of the testimony offered Monday by the State's witnesses.

"Outside of trivial disputes over rent and one occasion when Mosser attempted to put Miss Swann on his lap, there was, she stated, no trouble between them until the day of the shooting. She denied that she thought Mosser had informed Federal authorities that she was manufacturing liquor on his property. 'So help me heaven,' she cried, when Julius C. Renninger, State's Attorney of Garrett County, who is conducting the prosecution against her, questioned her about this matter, 'Mosser never mentioned my making moonshine. Why should he report me, when he made it himself on the place!'

"David A. Robb, one of the attorneys defending the accused, questioned her as to her past life. Educated in a private school and business school, she then worked several years for a wholesale millinery store in Baltimore, she said. Miss Swann, according to her testimony, then went in training as a nurse at Mercy Hospital, where she spent several years. Her last case was in

66

Westminister, Md., where she remained for a little over a year. On her return to Baltimore her health broke down, she stated.

"'My nerves were practically gone; I was a total wreck,' she told the court and jury. Because of her poor health, she declared, Baltimore physicians would not allow her to resume her nursing. Miss Swann then went to Fairmont, W.Va., according to her testimony, where she was employed as head waitress at a hotel for six years.

"Soon she bought a car, she said, and went into the taxi business, operating the machine herself. General farming near Fairmont occupied her time after this. Moving to Garrett County about three years ago, she rented various farms in this section, she said. All of the farm work, Miss Swann declared, was done by herself. Once in a while, during the harvesting season, she would hire help for a few days, according to her testimony.

"Prior to the time she rented the Mosser farm, she was engaged in general farming on the Rodeheaver estate, White's farm and the Charles Harvey from, all in Garrett County. She sold her produce in Oakland and Deer Park, she told the court and jury.

"Miss Swann first met Mosser the first week in February last, when she had an engagement with him at his farm to see about renting it from him. 'I got there about 10 o'clock in the morning,' she said. 'I knocked at the door. Somebody hollered "come in." I went in but saw no one. Dan was on the second floor.' The terms of the lease were then arranged and it was agreed that she could have the use of the farm for $125 a year, payments to be made quarterly, she said.

"Although Mosser agreed to repair the roof of the house and fix the fences on the farm, he never did it, she claimed. She moved in the following week--between the first and tenth of February. Including the first meeting when the terms of the lease were arranged, and the final meeting, when she shot and killed Mosser, she saw Mosser on the farm on six different occasions, she said.

"'Two or three weeks after I had moved in,' she declared, 'Mosser came to the farm, hunting a harness, he said. As it had been snowing and was cold, I asked him in. As I passed him on my way to the spring to get some water, he suddenly lunged at me and tried to pull me over on his lap. "God--you," he cried,

"I'll get you sooner or later.'" Nothing more happened, she said. Warding him off, she continued her way to the spring unmolested.

"When he came again several weeks later, Miss Swann testified, she asked him when he was going to make the repairs he had agreed to make. 'I'm not bothering about any repairs,' she quoted Mosser as saying, 'what I want is rent.' There had been a previous agreement, indirectly made between her and Mosser's sister in Cumberland, that she, Miss Swann, was not to pay Mosser the rent, as the family wanted it used to keep up the place, which, Miss Swann said, was in extremely poor shape.

"On another occasion, Miss Swann stated in her testimony, she returned to her farm, finding Mosser prowling about the house, pulling over chairs and bureaus, apparently looking for something.

"She was then questioned by Mr. Robb about the visit that Lawton Friend, Lester Shank, Russell Lee, Joseph Friend and Lester Weimer said they made to her farm on April 26 of this year. Miss Swann Monday was not certain of the date, but recalled the visit. The only one of the crowd whom she knew, she said, was Lawton Friend. They came up to her and Shank asked her if she had any 'hootch.'

"'I don't know what that means,' she replied.

"'Well, have you any moonshine?' she said Shank then asked her.

"'That depends,' Miss Swann told the court and jury.

"The young men then told her she had better get rid of the liquor, she testified, for, they said, the Federal officers were coming. Although she didn't believe it, she was finally persuaded by the young men to hide the liquor. They agreed to hide it for her, and a half barrel of mash was concealed in the woods nearby. The boys suggested that she give them a gallon for their services, which she did. It was nearly dark then, according to Miss Swann's story, and she returned to the hiding place of the liquor. It was gone, she declared.

"Miss Swann freely admitted making liquor, but she sold it, she said, only to one person. For the liquor she received credit on a bill of sale on her stock. Mr. Robb then asked her if she had made any threats against Mosser in her conversation with the young men. Receiving a negative reply, he asked her if she had ever made any threats against the dead man. She denied this also.

"The testimony of Peter Bickford, offered on Monday, was then called to her attention. Bickford alleged that she had told him that someone had raided her place, destroying her liquor. Bickford claimed that Miss Swann asked him if he thought it could have been Federal officers who had made the raid. When he said that it was more than probable, she told him that she had heard that Mosser informed the officers. 'If I find out, I'll kill him!' Bickford told the court and jury she said to him.

"Miss Swann, however, denied this in court Monday. She said that when she asked Bickford about the raid, he told her that he thought it was the 'hillbillies' of Swanton who had destroyed her liquor and not the revenue officers. Bickford advised her, she said Monday, to get out, as 'that bunch in Swanton isn't going to let you remain here.' Mosser's name was not mentioned at any time in the conversation, she said.

"On the day of the shooting, Miss Swann declared, she arose about 6:00 o'clock. Without eating any breakfast she went out on the farm to catch a heifer, which had escaped. She was washing up the breakfast dishes she said, when she heard the dogs barking outside. She paid no attention to them, however, and went on with her work. The door suddenly opened with a crash, she stated, and Mosser stood there. As the door was locked, he was forced to break it in. He asked for the rent, and she replied that she had none for him.

"'I'll have the rent or something,' Mosser growled as he left the room, Miss Swann said. Alarmed at his threatening appearance, she hurried to the kitchen to get the rifle. Returning to the living room, Mosser suddenly appeared in the doorway, and shouted, 'I'll have something,' and threw a brick at her and lunged in her direction. She held the rifle in one hand, and raising it, fired. Mosser paused, clutched his shoulder, wheeled around and staggered out. He went around the corner of the house, she said. Thoroughly excited and frightened, Miss Swann, with the gun still in her hand, went to the door of the house and called, 'Mosser.'

"She got no reply, and putting the gun down, ran for a horse. She then returned to the house, put the rifle in a dresser in the kitchen, and started for Swanton on the horse to summon aid,

69

she said.

"At this point there was considerable argument between the opposing attorneys. The State contended that Miss Swann should not be allowed to give as testimony any of the conversation between her and those whom she met at Swanton. Authorities were quoted and the trial was held up for some time while the court considered whether or not to sustain the objection raised by the State.

"Finally the court ruled that she would be allowed to give the disputed part of her testimony if it pertained to the case and was relevant. She first went to the home of Truman Sweitzer, she said, but finding no one there, continued to Crabtree Creek bridge. Here she met George D. Browning, a County Commissioner of Garrett County, Truman Sweitzer, Truman Mosser, an uncle of Daniel Mosser, Alex Mason and Robert Sheckells, who were occupied with some work at the bridge at the time.

"She told them about the shooting and asked them to summon a physician and the sheriff. She then returned to the farm where all was as she left it, she stated. An automobile and an unknown man were in the road. After that a number of people from Swanton arrived.

"Miss Swann was then turned over to the State. She was cross-examined closely by Julius C. Renninger, State's Attorney for Garrett County. He went over practically the same ground as Mr. Robb. She repeated her denials that there ever was any serious trouble between her and Mosser save on the day of the shooting. As she was a nurse, Mr. Renninger asked her, why didn't she administer aid to Mosser after she shot him.

"'I don't know,' she replied. 'I was too excited and scared, I guess. I didn't know what to do. Dan was lying outside, sort of huddled up.'

"At twenty minutes to three the State finished with Miss Swann and she was allowed to take her place at the table with her counsel.

"County Commissioner George D. Browning was called next. He told about Miss Swann coming to Crabtree Creek and asking for help. Robert Sheckells, a lumber dealer of Swanton, was the next witness. He also was present with Mr. Browning when Miss Swann arrived at the bridge in Swanton. His testimony was similar to Mr. Browning's.

70

"W.H. Lohr the foreman of the coroner's jury, the last witness called on Tuesday afternoon by the defense, declared that he saw the globe which the brick Mosser was said to have hurled at Miss Swann, and broke. He also told the court and jury that he noticed the unusual state of the door which Mosser is said to have broken in. The lock looked as if it had been forced, he declared, and the lock-keeper was not in its right place.

"Sheriff W.D. Casteel, who was summoned to the Mosser farm the day of the shooting, was the first witness for the State Tuesday morning. He told of his examination of the body. A pocketbook and a watch were found on the body, he said. Joy Griffith, deputy sheriff, also was recalled by the State Tuesday morning.

"Lester Weimer, 19, of Swanton who was with Joseph Friend, Luther Shank, Lawton Friend and Russell Lee when they visited Miss Swann's house on April 26, corroborated the testimony offered Monday by Shank and the Friends. He also heard Miss Swann make her alleged threat against Mosser, he said.

"Dr. Thomas Bess, of Keyser, W.Va., who performed an autopsy with other physicians on Mosser's body, was questioned about heart wounds.

"Mrs. Daniel Mosser, the widow of the dead man, was the last witness for the State.

Prosecution Ridicules

"The closing arguments for the State were opened at noon yesterday by E.R. Jones, who ridiculed Miss Swann's story of the shooting, which he said was a fabrication. The shooting, according to him, occurred outside the house. It was an unjustifiable murder, he said.

"The state of the door and the lock after the shooting, William A. Huster, Allegany County's State's Attorney asserted, indicated that they had been tampered with. The testimony of the defense, he asserted, was both ridiculous and unreliable. He asked for a verdict of guilty.

"The fact that the testimony offered by several physicians to the effect that the bullet had taken a downward course in Mosser's chest, showed, Mr. Renninger said, that he must have been shot while he was still outside the house. As there was a slight incline in front of the building, he stated, Mosser was shot while he was approaching. All the facts showed that Miss Swann had deliberately planned the act, he asserted.

"When Mosser came to the house on May 26, Miss Swann was lying in wait for him, Mr. Renninger said in closing his argument and asked for a verdict of murder in the first degree.

Defense Asks for Acquittal

"The defense contended that Miss Swann shot Mosser only after she had been provoked into doing it. Early on the morning of May 26, it was stated, Mosser came to the farm at Swanton, which Miss Swann leased from him, and demanded entrance to the house. When he was refused, it was claimed, he endeavored to force the door and threw a brick at her. His vile language and threatening manner, the defense asserted, forced her to shoot, without aiming, in order to frighten him away.

"Former Chief Judge William C. Walsh and William R. Offutt asked for an acquittal of their client. David A. Robb, who closed for the defense asked the court that if Miss Swann deliberately planned the murder, she would have secured a better weapon. The rifle which Miss Swann used in the killing was ridiculed. He asked for either a verdict of not guilty of first degree murder. 'No other verdict would fit the case,' he said.

"Chief Judge D. Lindley Sloan and Associate Judge Albert A. Doub were on the bench.

"A graduate of Mercy Hospital of Baltimore, Miss Swann, who had considerable nursing experience, came to this section several years ago for her health. When she appeared in court on Monday, evidence of the term she spent in jail showed plainly on her face. However, she seemed otherwise to be in excellent health and took a deep interest in the trial. She was calm and smiled faintly at the testimony offered by the various witnesses. She was dressed neatly in a black dress and brown hat, with a string of pearls around her neck. Her only sister, from Baltimore, sat beside her during the trial.

Swann Found Guilty of
Murder in Second Degree

"A verdict of murder in the second degree was rendered at 10:20 o'clock this morning (10/27/27) in the case of Mabel Swann, 43, former Baltimore nurse, accused of the murder of Daniel Mosser, her landlord, on May 26, near the town of Swanton, by a jury which had been deadlocked since five o'clock yesterday evening at Cumberland. The jury in rendering its verdict asked that leniency be shown the convicted woman when she is called to be sentenced by the court.

"The trial, which began early Monday morning, was hotly contested by both sides. The trial attracted many people, the courtroom being crowded to capacity with spectators all the time the case was in progress.

"There were thirty-two witnesses for the State, including those who were on the scene immediately after the shooting, physicians who examined the body of Mosser, and Sheriff Casteel and his deputy, Joy Griffith.

"The fate of Mabel Swann rested with the jury until 10:20 o'clock this morning, which body remained at the court house from 5:00 o'clock yesterday afternoon until midnight without reaching a verdict. It was rumored that one member of the jury held out against the others of the body, which prevented the early rendering of the decision of the body. At midnight the jury was taken to a hotel in Cumberland where they remained until this morning.

Swann Sentenced to
Three Years in Prison

"Mabel Swann who was convicted by a jury last Friday of murder in the second degree for shooting and fatally wounding her landlord, Daniel Mosser, at her home in Swanton, was given a sentence of three years in the Maryland penitentiary by Chief Judge D.D. Lindley Sloan of Cumberland, shortly after two o'clock Monday afternoon. She was taken Tuesday morning to the Maryland penitentiary. Later she will be moved to the House of Correction. She heard the verdict pronounced without untoward movement and she remained composed.

"Miss Swann was given a physical examination Monday morning by Dr. W.E. Williams, county physician, and Dr. A.H. Hawkins, who submitted a report to the court. Judge Sloan, before passing sentence, declared that the physicians had found Miss Swann suffering from toxic goiter, which will, sooner or later, have to be given medical attention. An immediate operation would be advisable, Judge Sloan said the physicians believed.

"However, Judge Sloan stated that it would not be fair to Miss Swann to make her undergo an operation at present, as she could begin immediately to serve her time. Later, if it is so desired, he said, steps may be taken toward such an operation.

"Since the jury had recommended mercy in its verdict, Judge Sloan said, the court felt that such a recommendation should be carried out to its fullest extent. The court had, he declared, conducted a thorough investigation into the woman's past and the result showed that she had never been guilty of immorality. 'The finger of shame has never been pointed at her,' Judge Sloan said. Her excellent character, her poor health and the jury's recommendation, he asserted, made a light sentence the only fair one.

"He then passed sentence. Miss Swann, who had been brought into the court room at 2:15 o'clock, obviously in a state of extreme agitation, received the sentence calmly. She immediately began consulting her attorney, David A. Robb, who assisted in her defense. About five minutes later, she was taken out of the court room and back to the jail. Mr. Robb asked the court to be lenient in its sentence. The jury, he said, apparently made a compromise in order to reach its verdict. The testimony of the State, in his opinion, was valueless in several places, especially in that part which made threats against the life of Mosser. As an officer of the court and not her counsel, he said, he was firmly convinced that Miss Swann's life had been that of a good though eccentric woman. Closing, he said she had been 'guessed into a conviction.'

"Miss Swann's trial started last Monday and ended late Thursday afternoon. She was charged with shooting and killing her landlord, Daniel Mosser, near Swanton. The defense contended that she had shot Mosser in order to protect her life. The State asserted that she had murdered Mosser because she thought he had informed Federal officers that she was making liquor on her place.

Mabel Swann Will Get Parole For Operation

"Because a prompt operation is the only measure to save the life of Miss Mabel Swann, serving a three-year term in the Maryland House of Correction, for the killing of Daniel Mosser near Swanton last May, Governor Ritchie announced on Tuesday that he would grant her a temporary parole according to a February 2, 1928 newspaper article.

"Miss Swann, according to physicians who attended her while she was a prisoner in the Garrett County jail awaiting trial, is suffering from a goiter growth. The local physicians' diagnosis has been borne out by the opinion of the House of Correction medical men who reported to the executive department and because there are no facilities at the penal institution for the performance of the necessary operation, the governor agreed to parole her until she had recovered.

"The matter of releasing the woman had met with the approval of State's Attorney Huster, of Allegany County, who prosecuted the case, and State's Attorney Renninger, of Garrett County, prosecutor in the county where the slaying took place.

"Miss Swann was convicted of having shot and killed Mosser when the man was said to have attempted to break into her home, which was the farmhouse on the Mosser place jointly owned by Daniel Mosser and other heirs and which was leased to Miss Swann. At the trial she entered a plea of self-defense, but a jury found her guilty of second degree murder on October 31, 1927, when she was sentenced to the House of Correction for three years' imprisonment.

"The woman will be paroled in the custody of her mother, and will not be forced to return to serve out her sentence until her health has sufficiently improved following the operation, it was announced at the office of the Maryland Governor.

"Miss Swann was tried and convicted during the October term of Allegany County Circuit Court. Her case was moved from Garrett County when the contention was entered that she would not get a fair trial in Garrett County.

"At the time she was sentenced to three years' imprisonment the Court's attention was called to the fact that she was suffering from goiter, but it was pointed out that, if necessary, provision could be made for her to undergo an operation after she began serving her term.

"State's Attorney Huster of Allegany County, when notified by Governor Ritchie of the contemplated parole of Miss Swann informed the Governor that he believed the lightness of the woman's sentence was due to her physical condition. Mr. Huster told the Governor also, it is said, that he had no objection to Miss Swann being released to undergo an operation and then being returned to the House of Correction. However, he pointed out that as the case originated in Garrett County he did not feel that he should make any recommendation in the matter and it should be referred to State's Attorney Renninger of Oakland.

"When the matter was referred to State's Attorney Renninger by the Governor he told the executive that he saw no objection in granting a temporary parole to Miss Swann to allow her to enter a hospital for the operation, but it was understood that the parole was only a temporary one, and that she had to be returned to the House of Correction after she had undergone the operation and regained her strength."

(From a February 2, 1928 article. The newspaper was researched thru the remainder of the year; no proof was found that Miss Swann was returned to the House of Correction.)

The Green Glades Tavern

"John Hays, a Virginian, soon after the Old Road was opened (about 1789) settled along it in the Green Glade area, building a big log house in which he lived and kept an inn, 'The Green Glades Tavern,' a noted road house during many years. In 1809, he deeded the property to James Morrison for $1,000. The son-in-law of Morrison, Henry Ingman, b. 1777-1779, moved to the tavern and operated it for a long time although he never owned it. He and his wife are buried on the place together with some of the Hamills and other neighbors. No sign of the inn or cemetery exists today.

"In 1824, John C. Calhoun, the Secretary of War, stopped at the tavern with a party of engineers overnight. The tavern was near the summit level of the proposed trans-mountain canal. It was planned to make a deep cut or dig a tunnel thru the divide from the waters of Crabtree Creek to Green Glade Run, and by locks lift and lower canal boats up and down the mountain side. A century later work was begun on a dam across Deep Creek. A similar dam was included in the engineering plans for the canal.

"The tavern was kept by a man named Kight after Ingman's time. It was torn down about 1890.

"James Male is said to have been residing there when his wife cut off his head with an axe, because while drunk he had threatened to beat her. Perhaps because of this and other deeds of violence, the place was said to be haunted." (*Dennis Rasche, April 17, 1962*).

Note: The Inn was located on the property now owned by Mr. Herman Steiding, Steiding Church Road, near Turkey Neck. The inn sat on the right side going in his farm lane. In a conversation with Mr. Steiding, he stated that whenever he plowed the field where the Inn had been located, he often uncovered various items and pieces of relics in that area, and had once uncovered an andiron from the old Inn. No remains of the Inn or the cemetery can be seen today. (*Martha Kahl, April 7, 1974*).